Story Play:

Building Language and Literacy
One Story at a Time

by Mary Jo Huff

Dedication and Acknowledgments

Our world is filled with wonderful people and connecting stories. This book is for all the children, teachers, librarians, child care specialists, professors, presenters, audiences, and special friends—Vanessa, Jerry, Susan, Lisa Kay, Pam, Clarissa, Sharon, Jim, Georgiana, John, Connie, Sue, Jane, Carol, Lorna, Gay, Barb, Pat—and my special listening family Sissy, Bill, Cathy, Kenny, Joe, Nikki, Melody, John, Kurt, Melanie, Matt, Michael, Eli, Liam, and Cole. Each story we share is a stepping stone from the past to the future.

Special thanks to Darrell's Photography in Newburgh, Indiana, for the wonderful photographs in this book and to the staff and children at St. John Kinder Kountry Pre-School in Newburgh, Indiana.

To everyone who knows me I say, "Thanks for listening!"

A MARY JO HUFF BOOK

Story Play

Building Language and Literacy One Story at a Time

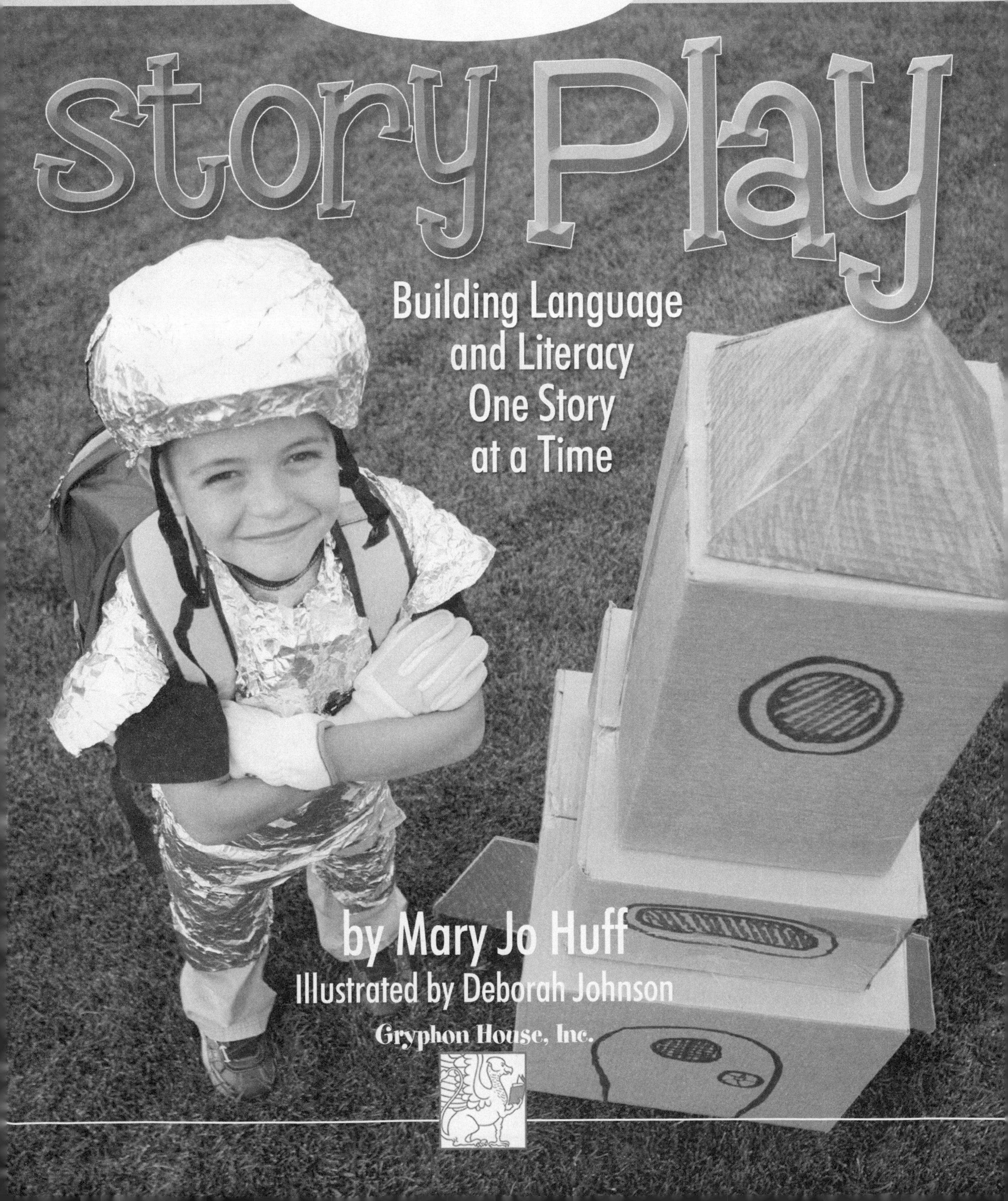

by Mary Jo Huff

Illustrated by Deborah Johnson

Gryphon House, Inc.

©2011 Mary Jo Huff
Published by Gryphon House, Inc.
10770 Columbia Pike, Suite 201
Silver Spring, MD 20901 | 301.595.9500
301.595.0051 (fax); 800.638.0928 (toll-free)

Visit us on the web at www.gryphonhouse.com.

Bulk purchase

Gryphon House books are available for special premiums and sales promotions as well as for fund-raising use. Special editions or book excerpts also can be created to specification. For details, contact the Director of Marketing at Gryphon House.

Disclaimer

Gryphon House, Inc. and the author cannot be held responsible for damage, mishap, or injury incurred during the use of or because of activities in this book. Appropriate and reasonable caution and adult supervision of children involved in activities, and corresponding to the age and capability of each child involved, is recommended at all times. Do not leave children unattended at any time. Observe safety and caution at all times.

Every effort has been made to locate copyright and permission information.

Cover Photograph: © iStockphoto LP 2009. All rights reserved. iStockphoto® and iStock® are trademarks of iStockphoto LP. Flash® is a registered trademark of Adobe Inc. www.istockphoto.com.

Illustrated by Deborah Johnson.

Library of Congress Cataloging-in-Publication Data

Huff, Mary Jo.
 Story play : building language and literacy one story at a time / by Mary Jo Huff.
    p. cm.
 Includes index.
 ISBN 978-0-87659-316-5
 1. Storytelling. 2. Storytelling ability in children. 3. Literacy—Study and teaching (Primary)—Activity programs. 4. Language arts (Primary)—Activity programs. I. Title.
 LB1042.H78 2011
 372.67'7--dc22
                          2010023383

Table of Contents

Many of the songs and chants in this book are featured on the following CDs by Mary Jo Huff:

Chicken Fun
Getting Loose with Mother Goose
Peeper Pizzaazzz
Storytelling for Kids!

For more storytelling fun, view the following DVDs:
Fairy Tales, Fantasy, and Storytellin' Fun
Storytelling: Tips, Techniques, and Tools

Foreword

by Pam Schiller

Next time you attend a family gathering, listen to people talking and you are likely to hear stories. Maybe not the "once upon a time" type of story but stories nonetheless—anecdotes about family members' lives or about the people they know. Now listen to children while they are playing, inside with toys or outside on the playground. Children are filled with stories—some real, some make-believe. Storytelling is older than formal language. It began with drawings and gestures: it is a core component of communication. You will be hard-pressed to spend a day that does not include telling and listening to stories.

With the push for early literacy, teachers and caregivers have become focused on using books to develop literacy skills. This focus has all but eliminated storytelling in most classrooms. Yet research is clear that comprehension is more than just understanding and reading stories in books. It is optimized when children have the experience of listening to stories, can participate in the telling of stories, and have opportunities to retell stories.

The wonderful collection of stories and activities in this book encourages all this and, at the same time, adds joy to learning. Mary Jo Huff is a gifted storyteller and a knowledgeable literacy expert who uses her intuitive sense of what appeals to children to bring old stories, sometimes with a new twist, such as "Little Boy Blue" and "Hickety Pickety," and new stories, such as "Shirley and Sam" or "Spider Soup," into their hearts. I am honored to have been asked to write the foreword for this book. It will be an invaluable asset to every teacher of young children. As these stories and activities come alive in the classroom, children will develop those all-important comprehension skills and receive a treasure they will hold for life—a love of stories.

Introduction

Light a fire in a child's imagination!

Stories never get old, but they do change their flavor as they are told and retold. This book is filled with ideas that will enhance the storytelling experience in your classroom. As you share the activities; sing songs; use props and puppets; and tell poems; the children in your classroom will become actively engaged in the storytelling process. The new flavors you and the children bring to the stories will promote communication and language development across the curriculum. This book will help you learn how to decide which stories to share in your classroom; how to use those stories to develop specific literacy skills; and how to enhance those stories by presenting the characters, setting, plot, and resolution in a way that makes all of it relevant to the lives of the children in your care.

Experiences with oral and written language provide a solid foundation for early literacy. "During the first years and months of life, a child's experiences with language and literacy begin to form a basis for their later reading success. Research consistently demonstrates that the more children know about language and literacy before they arrive at school, the better equipped they are to succeed in reading" (*Starting Out Right: A Guide to Promoting Reading Success*, National Research Council, 1999).

This book will help you guide children as they interact with familiar stories. You will also explore how to engage children in redirecting the story by changing some of the main elements. As the children become more familiar with everyday stories, take the time to discuss the characters, settings, plots, and resolutions of the stories, and ask the children how they would make changes. Document their changes on a chart and you will find that you have created a new story from the original.

Working with the ideas in this book will help you to develop, practice, and improve children's:

* Imaginations
* Oral communication skills
* Auditory discrimination
* Listening and pre-reading skills
* Creativity
* Fine motor skills
* Visual discrimination
* Critical thinking skills
* Sequencing skills

In addition, this book will help children develop a love of books, reading, and, eventually, writing.

On page 148 you will find a form to help you record your favorite stories and connect those stories to your curriculum. This form can be filled out for each of your stories and kept for documentation and demonstration of how a story addresses many areas of the curriculum. The form also has a place for you to add additional ideas as you find props, puppets, poems, fingerplays, chants, and other stories to support each favorite story.

When a story comes to "The End," it may be the end of the story, but it should be the beginning of an expanded conversation: a continuation of the storytelling experience. This book will give you ideas and strategies to help you find the storyteller within yourself. By enriching your storytelling in creative and imaginative new ways, you will guide children to discover the magic and enchantment of hearing a story and the joy of creating new stories. You will also find yourself enjoying the stories more as the children learn how to tell stories, sing stories, and play with stories.

Storytelling, Language, and Literacy

Storytelling:
Educational Brain Food

Storytelling in the preschool classroom might best be described as providing educational food for the brain.

Storytelling:

* Creates an intimate connection between the teller and the listener.
* Offers room for spontaneity and feeling as the storyteller adds her own personality to the story.
* Provides opportunities for children, as listeners, to improve their comprehension skills and to use their imaginations to form the stories in their own minds.
* Enhances literacy skills such as vocabulary development and phonemic awareness as children consistently hear and learn to recognize new words.
* Exposes children to new ideas as they hear stories they have never heard before. They set out on a new adventure every time they are engaged in a storytelling experience.
* Connects reading, writing, and speaking as children realize that what they have heard can be written, and what has been written can be read and heard. Reading improves writing and writing improves reading.

✳ Creates logical connections. As children hear and understand stories, they learn sequencing skills, about cause and effect, how to predict what might come next, how to evaluate what they have heard, and how to role play.

Story Classifications

Throughout the centuries, stories have served a purpose that goes beyond simple entertainment. The following paragraphs describe and explain various kinds of stories.

Fables—Short tales that have a moral and communicate a truth about life. The main characters in fables are often animals that act and think like humans. These stories have a moral ending. Aesop's fables are probably the most famous of this type of story. These include stories such as "The Ant and the Grasshopper," "The Town Mouse and the Country Mouse," and "The Tortoise and the Hare."

Fairy Tales—Stories that often include fairies, elves, genies, pixies, leprechauns, and other make-believe characters. They are sometimes called *magic stories* and usually have a *happily ever after* ending. "Thumbelina," "Sleeping Beauty," and "Cinderella" are all well-known fairy tales.

Legends—Stories that revolve around incidents that are believed to have taken place in a particular culture's history. The stories of Robin Hood and Pocahontas are legends many children already know.

Folk Tales—Stories that come to us from many parts of the world. These stories reflect a particular country or people and preserve cultural traditions. Folk tales sometimes explain life and nature using talking animals. The stories of Paul Bunyan and Pecos Bill are North American folk tales.

Familiarize yourself with different types of stories and use the form provided on page 148 in this book to keep a record of the stories you enjoy telling. Starting with a simple record-keeping system will lead to categorizing your collection as time goes on. Create a three-ring binder with tabs using the story classification categories and add your own categories as your storytelling list increases.

Storytelling Tips

* Find that special story. What makes a story special depends on many things, including you, the children in your care, and the area where you live. A story might remind you of your own childhood, reflect the culture of the children in your class, or take place in a setting similar to your hometown. Enlist the help of family members in recording their stories and invite them into the classroom to share with the children. All of these things make the story special and help the children connect it with their own lives.

* Your local library is a good source for children's books written by local authors.

* Learn the beginning and the end of a story. Now, think about ways you can change the story in the middle to create a new story, teach a new skill, or aid in the children's development.

* Be flexible and creative. Change the story as you tell it in order to make it more meaningful to the listeners. For example, if you live on the West Coast, Goldilocks could be traveling down the beach and find the Bear family's house in a cliffside cave.

* Practice the story by telling it aloud until you are comfortable with it.

* Use voice inflections. Talk in high, low, squeaky, funny, gnarly, and other voices.

* Move your body. Explore the parts of the story that invite you to use body movement.

* Be sure the children are sitting so they can see you.

- Introduce the story; do not just jump into the telling. Set the scene by saying something about the story. For example, before beginning the story of "Little Red Riding Hood," you might ask the children if they have ever been in the woods. Ask them to tell you their own experiences. Then you could say, "I know a story about a little girl who went into the woods and had an adventure."
- Look for places in the story where the audience can participate.
- Add music, humor, magic, and puppets to the story.
- Prepare props that will enhance the story. For example, use stuffed bears in three different sizes to tell the story of "Goldilocks and the Three Bears" or a simple piece of red fabric as the red cape in "Little Red Riding Hood."
- Tell the story and watch the eyes of the children as you are telling the story. You will know if they are engaged with the story or not. Asking another teacher to sit with restless children often helps them focus. If the children are restless, introduce movement into the story. For example, get up and walk through the "forest" (the classroom) if the children get restless when you are telling them the story of "Little Red Riding Hood."
- Children like to hear the same story more than once, so be prepared to hear them say, "Tell it again!"

Storytelling Connections

Building a Foundation

It is important to know the stories you will tell. Learn the beginning, middle, and end of each story along with the characters and settings that connect the problem and solution. Young children enjoy talking about a story and changing the story with a "what if." As long as the beginning and ending remain consistent, there is no limit to what can happen in the middle.

Simple Stories and Connections

Young children need to grasp the plot and visualize the characters and setting to engage with the story. Simple stories are best when they come at the beginning of a child's experience with storytelling. After telling a story, provide opportunities for children to connect with the story through their own play. For example, add clothing and props to the Dramatic Play Center, related art materials to the Art Center, related music CDs to the Music Center, and so on. These things help children connect the story to the activities they are doing throughout the day.

Image Making

When children hear a story, they create images in their minds based on what they already know. This is the way they connect with the setting, a character, or a problem in the story. Invite children to expand their imaginations further by asking them to describe the three little pigs and the big bad wolf or any other story characters, or by asking them to draw a picture about the story.

Learning to create mental images when listening to a story develops into being able to create images when reading a story. Some children can imagine an entire story, while others can imagine only one word or phrase. Enjoy the conversation and take the lead from the children. If they seem to need more clues to help them create the scene in their minds, you can provide additional information.

Story Making

When children begin to tell their own stories, compliment their story making and challenge them to go further with their stories. Show & Tell, for example, can become a storytelling event for all ages. Instead of a whole class having Show & Tell, consider having a specific child assigned daily as the Show & Tell story maker. Rotate this assignment and keep a visual record in the classroom such as a chart or graph. Children will soon become familiar with talking in front of their peers and telling their own stories.

Relationship of Language and Learning

Storytelling invites children to share what is on their minds in a non-threatening way that makes them feel comfortable. Often there is a treasure trove of thoughts just beneath the surface of a child's story. If you take the time to listen, you will discover what is on their minds, in their imaginations, and in their hearts.

Dramatic Interpretation

All children enjoy dramatizing a story. Encourage children to become part of the story. Use the Storytelling Helper (page 31) or Story Basket (page 34) to choose the children to participate in the day's storytelling. Provide musical instruments, costumes, and other props for children to create their own characters.

Participation

Find stories that have phrases, musical chants, repeated words, and actions for the children. Give children the opportunity to be a part of the story and they will ask for the same story to be repeated again and again. As children participate, they are engaged in real learning while enhancing their language skills.

Creating a Storytelling Environment in the Classroom

To create a fun and educational storytelling environment in the classroom, certain elements are helpful, though not absolutely necessary.

Puppets

Puppets are a powerful way to reach children. Even shy children will relate to a puppet. Puppets can be vehicles for storytelling and will create a connection to the storytelling experience that children can understand. A class mascot puppet is a tremendous helper in the Story

Corner. A mascot can be used during a challenging situation to share a message of how to deal with that situation. Puppets draw the children's attention and can help start and finish a story session.

Props

Props make a story come alive! Using props allows you to go beyond simply reading a story to create a lively and educational listening experience. Props help children visualize what they are hearing, making it easier for them to retell a story after hearing it. In addition, as children use and manipulate the props, they develop their fine motor skills and gain a stronger connection to the story. This allows them to remember and retell it more effectively.

Using Velcro™

Velcro comes in self-sticking strips, squares, and dots; in self-sticking tape form; and in wide widths that can be glued, sewn, and stapled. If you do not want to use Velcro and a Storyboard (see below), you can use magnetic tape and cookie sheets. Just make sure the magnetic tape is firmly attached to the figures. For flexibility, you might want to consider attaching both a piece of magnetic tape and a piece of Velcro hook to each item. (Be sure to place the magnet above the Velcro.) This gives you the flexibility to work in different storytelling modes.

Storyboard

A Storyboard is similar to a flannel board. Cover any type of lightweight board (such as an old flannel board) with soft-sided Velcro fabric called loop (available at specialty fabric stores). This provides a surface for storytelling with story characters. You can cut art foam into shapes that relate to the stories; these shapes, as well as laminated figures and characters you create, can be used with the Storyboard by attaching Velcro hook tape to the backs of the items.

Create a simple Storyboard by taking a piece of the Velcro fabric and folding it to the size desired. Sew the two sides and leave the bottom open, similar to a pillowcase. Measure the intended board so the new cover is good and tight. Slip the cover over any old flannel board for a new and exciting experience.

Story Wall

Many classrooms are required to have word walls. A Story Wall expands on this concept and is an advantage for children who need visual clues about the day's story. Create a Story Wall by covering a bulletin board or part of a wall with flannel or Velcro loop fabric. (Be sure that the children can reach the Story Wall.) Copy pictures from a favorite book, add Velcro hook, and attach to the Story Wall. Copy the cover of the book, laminate it, attach Velcro, and display it with pictures and words from the story. Children can visit the Story Wall and use the materials to retell the story. The use of Velcro allows the Story Wall items to be easily manipulated. Experiencing familiar stories in this new and interactive way builds a strong foundation for oral and visual language.

Story Box

A Story Box is a simple box (copy paper box or file box with handles) that holds stories that are personal to the class. You can use the Story Box at circle time, at small group time, or with one or two children in a storytelling center, library center, or literacy center.

Suggest that the children decorate the box. After the box is decorated, ask the children to help you write a story about the class. Keep this story in the box. Invite the children to add their own stories to the box. Send a note home with the children asking their families to write a story about something they did as a family. It can be about a special time, such as a vacation or trip, or about time spent with someone special, such as a relative, friend, or neighbor. Or it might be a story about something else meaningful to them, such as a pet or a favorite stuffed animal. Place all the stories in the Story Box.

Pick a time to open the box and read a story. Don't say whose story it is. Instead, ask the class to guess who the story is about. Then suggest that children can write their own stories about the same subject (or something else important to them) and put them in their story bags (see below) to take home. You can use this idea throughout the year to connect the children's families with what going on in the classroom.

Story Bags

Each child should have his own story bag. You can use paper bags, but it is better to use a stronger paper or cloth bag with handles, so the bags are easy to carry and can be stored on a hook in the classroom. Ask each child to decorate one bag. Label it with the child's name or with "[child's name]'s Special Story Bag." They can use this bag to take stories (see Story Box, above) and story items back and forth from school to home.

Storytelling Tool Box

Decorate a tool box with theme-related or seasonal drawings, stickers, or paint, and fill it with props to use when telling stories. Some suggested items for the box are: child-safe scissors for cut-and-tell stories, a pen for draw-and-tell stories, puppets, a kazoo, a harmonica, felt story characters, finger puppets, and any other storytelling props.

Use the Storytelling Tool Box to challenge the children's imaginations. Invite them to guess what is in the box at group time, story time, or during the morning message time. Children are usually so curious to find out what is in the box that they become quiet and eager to find out what will come next.

Another idea is to provide a Storytelling Tool Box that the children can use to tell or retell stories. Provide finger puppets and any other story-related props for the children to use to tell or retell a story. Change the items often. A Storytelling Tool Box is often so compelling that children gather together and share a story experience without any suggestions from you.

Storytelling Apron

A Storytelling Apron can be purchased from many educational supply stores or catalogs. Storytelling Aprons are worn like typical aprons, usually have pockets, and are made of material that props or items stick to easily. The pockets provide a handy place to store the characters and small props to be used for a story. When you wear the apron and place the props or characters on the apron as you tell the story, children experience the story in an active way. To use a Storytelling Apron effectively, each prop or item that you use must have Velcro attached to the back.

Storytelling Aprons allow for mobility and are especially effective with younger children. With a Storytelling Apron, you can move from side to side or all around the room while showing and telling the story. As the characters in the story emerge from the apron pockets, the children get more and more intrigued by the story and the characters in it. Storytelling Aprons are adjustable to fit most people. They are washable, and storage is simple because an apron can be hung on a hook in the Story Corner or placed in a bag with story characters so it is ready at any time. The apron can also be used to work with colors, shapes, and numbers for categorizing, matching, and sorting. No classroom should be without this valuable educational tool.

Story Mitt

A Story Mitt is an exceptional tool to use with two-character stories. Some examples are "The Lion and the Mouse," "The Tortoise and the Hare," and any other story with two characters. Find pictures representing familiar characters in magazines, cut them out, and laminate them. Attach a piece of Velcro to the characters, and you are ready to tell a story. Attach the characters as you tell the story. You can easily use both sides of the mitt by rotating your hand. This simple tool fascinates children, and you are guaranteed to have their attention.

Story Bands

Story Bands are 2" wide pieces of loop-sided Velcro fabric cut in approximately 30" strips. Attach a piece of Velcro hook tape to one end of the fabric on the non-loop side so each band attaches to itself when placed around the upper chest of a child (under the arms).

Create story characters with art foam, glossy card stock paper, magazine pictures, stiff felt, or any other material you find that can be attached with Velcro. Attach each character to a Story Band, making the children an active part of the storytelling experience.

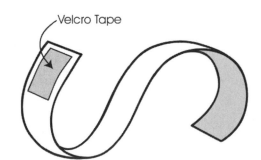

Velcro Tape

The bands are a must-have for children to act out stories. They are free to move, dance, wiggle, and get into character. The Story Bands can be used for stories, poems, chants, songs, or any other way you find to get children involved with language.

Pizza Story Box

Measure a pizza box (all sizes work well) and cut a piece of loop-sided Velcro fabric to fit inside the box lid. Glue the fabric to the inside of the lid. This provides a surface for attaching characters and scenery that have Velcro hook on the back. Decorate the outside of the box to connect with a theme or project. Place story characters inside the box and label the outside. These story boxes can be used at story time, circle time, or as a part of everyday center activities.

When labeling the outside of the box, add a picture of one of the story characters for children who need a visual connection.

Napkin Book

Buy colorful, thematic, decorated napkins in specialty stores, party stores, card shops, or local discount stores. Small napkins are an ideal size to make books for young children; adults can make books with larger napkins. The books will be almost indestructible, and they are easy to wipe clean. Consider making class books that match the children's take-home books.

Make a Napkin Book by unfolding a napkin once, so you have a rectangle with one long folded edge. Laminate the napkin with a 3 mm laminate. Insert the napkin, fold-side first, into the laminating machine. Once it has been laminated, cut around the edges, leaving a ¼" border of laminate around the edge of the napkin. Fold it in half again on the original fold line. Now you have the front and back cover for your book!

Cut four or five sheets of colored paper to a size just slightly smaller than the size of the unfolded cover. Fold these cut sheets in half and place them inside the front and back covers to make the pages of the book. Use a push pin (an adult-only step) to poke three holes, evenly spaced, along the folded edge of the pages and the cover. Be sure you go through all the layers of paper and plastic. Using these pre-punched holes, you can sew the pages inside the book with yarn and a blunt yarn needle. If you prefer, you can staple the pages into the Napkin Books with a strong stapler that does not leave the sharp points of the staples sticking out. (One-Touch™ or PaperPro® are two models that work well.)

Note: This idea can be used with any theme, special story, or topic you are teaching. For example, use apples in September, pumpkins in October, turkeys in November, and so on.

Story Corner

The Story Corner should communicate that it is a special place to play with language. It should clearly indicate that this is the place where story play begins, so that as children enter this special place they are ready to listen to a story as it is told or read. Storytelling involves cooperation and interaction, which, in turn, promotes literacy and love of language. Children who experience interactive

storytelling develop a solid foundation on which to build future reading and writing skills.

A well-equipped Story Corner should contain:

* Books
* Magnetic board
* Music, either a CD player or iPod™ with speakers
* Musical instruments
* Props
* Puppets
* Storyboard
* Storyboard characters
* Storytelling Apron
* Tape recorder

Seating

The storyteller can stand in front of or sit with the group of children. Adults are often encouraged to sit on the same level as the children (for example, on the floor if they are on the floor, in a chair if they are in chairs), but it will be easier for all the children to see the storyteller if you sit a bit above the children. The seat you use can be a decorated swivel stool, a decorated short stool, a rocking chair, a simple bench, or a decorated straight-backed chair. Find what works the best for you and the children in your classroom. The listeners can sit on a special story rug, the floor, a quilt, or a story sheet (see below). As you become more adept at storytelling, you will find the seating arrangement that best enables the children to connect with the story.

Story Sheet

At a time when the children are not in the classroom, spray paint an ordinary cotton sheet to create a special atmosphere. Paint a sheet that looks like the sky filled with white clouds when telling the story of the book *It Looked Like Spilt Milk.* Paint other sheets to match the seasons. They are easy to store and create a pleasant visual effect.

Story Rug

When there is a rug in the storytelling area, children will automatically sit on it for story time. Encouraging the children to sit in a group rather than in a semicircle creates a cozier environment for the storytelling experience.

Story Organization

Include a story file in the Story Corner. File folders can be stored in portable storage boxes. Create one folder for each story, in which you place a copy of the story, a list of the props used, and the storyboard characters. If you store your stories on your computer, keep a hard copy in the storytelling area. Computer files should include a copy of the story, a list of the props used, and printable templates of the storyboard characters.

Education Standards

Standards have become a hallmark of education today. Many preschool programs now require teachers to reference state standards in their curriculum. While this book does not address standards directly, you will find a space for recording standards on the Story Record Form on page 148.

More information on how this book and other books published by Gryphon House meet education standards can be found on Gryphon House's website at gryphonhouse.com.

The National Association for the Education of Young Children (NAEYC) and the National Association of Early Childhood Specialists in State Departments of Education (NAECS-SDE) each have position statements concerning standards for early childhood education posted on their websites (naeyc.org and naecs-sde.org). The National Council of Teachers of English (NCTE) provides a set of standards on their website (ncte.org). The Head Start Outcomes Framework is a set of standards used by Head Start teachers in their classrooms, which you will find at the website hsnrc.org.

Storytelling Helpers

Storytelling Helper Can

What the Children Will Learn

* To recognize their names
* To take turns

Materials

card stock paper (cut into 3" × 5" pieces) or index cards

permanent marker

spray paint in two different colors (adult use only)

two empty one-pound coffee cans or any type of can
that can be painted

vinyl letters or black paint

Preparation

✳ Use spray paint to color two cans, each a different color. This should be done when no children are present.

✳ Use the vinyl letters or black paint to label each can. Label one can "Storytelling Helper #1" and the other "Storytelling Helper #2."

✳ Print each child's name on a piece of card stock paper or an index card.

✳ Place all the name cards in the first can.

What to Do

1. When you need a storytelling helper, draw a child's name from the first can. Read the child's name.

2. Ask this child to put her name card in the second can. It will stay there until the first can is empty, which ensures that each child gets a turn as helper.

3. When the second can is full, put all the name cards back in the first can and start again.

4. As the year progresses, add the children's last names to the name cards. Stickers and special designs can be added to support seasonal and thematic units.

Reviewing What the Children Learned

✳ Place all the name cards on a table and ask one child to find her name card and to identify the name cards of other children in the class.

More to Do

✳ Make a second set of name cards using a different color marker. Take the name cards from the Storytelling Helper Can and use them with the second set to play a memory matching game.

�֍ Ask the day's storytelling helper to create a drawing of the day's story. Display this picture on a bulletin board under the heading "Our Storytelling Helper's Illustration." Post a written version of the story alongside the picture. If the story is too long, post a short synopsis.

Related Books

Andy, That's My Name by Tomie dePaola
The Name Jar by Yangsook Choi

Story Basket

What the Children Will Learn

- To experiment with language
- To use their imaginations to create new ideas from familiar rhymes

Materials

card stock paper or 4" × 6" index cards
markers
small or medium basket

Preparation

- Create cards by printing the names of familiar nursery rhymes on the card stock (cut into 4" × 6" cards) or the index cards. Some rhymes to consider are "Mary Had a Little Lamb;" "Jack Be Nimble;" "Diddle, Diddle, Dumpling, My Son John;" "Hey! Diddle, Diddle;" "Hickory, Dickory, Dock;" "Humpty-Dumpty;" "Jack and Jill;" "Little Bo-Peep;" "Little Boy Blue;" "Little Miss Muffet;" and similar nursery rhymes.
- Place the cards in the basket.

What to Do

1. During story time, choose a card from the Storytelling Helper Can (see page 31) and a card from the Story Basket. Lead the group in saying the rhyme on the card.
2. For variety, change the rhyme. Use the Storytelling Helper's name instead of the character's name in the rhyme; change the location where the rhyme takes place (Little Miss Muffet sat on a windowsill); or change something about the character, such as making the lamb's fleece green (or pink or purple) instead of white.

Reviewing What the Children Learned

✖ Ask individual children to recall certain elements from the rhyme of the day.

More to Do

✖ Provide collage materials that are relevant to the rhyme (cotton puffs for lambs, flower pictures for "Mistress Mary," candle and flame cutouts for "Jack Be Nimble"). Encourage the children to use the materials to create illustrations for the rhyme of the day.

✖ Add some props to the Dramatic Play Center that support the rhyme chosen that day. Encourage the children to use the props to act out the rhyme.

Related Books

Cecily Parsley's Nursery Rhymes by Beatrix Potter

A Child's Treasury of Nursery Rhymes by Kady MacDonald Denton

Favorite Nursery Rhymes from Mother Goose by Scott Gustafson

A Treasury of African American ABC's and Nursery Rhymes for Children by Michelle L. Washington

Story Clues

Materials

card stock paper

glue or glue sticks

mounting materials (tape, sticky tack, and other mounting materials)

pictures representing items from the day's story

scissors (adult use only)

Preparation

✗ Use magazines, old books, or clipart to find pictures that represent elements of the day's story. For instance, if your story will be "Goldilocks and the Three Bears," then a picture of blonde hair would be a good story clue. For the story *Koala Lou* by Mem Fox, a picture of a koala is appropriate. For the nursery rhyme "Humpty Dumpty," a photo of a carton of eggs should get the children thinking.

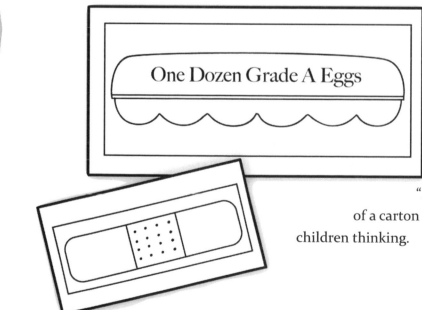

* Mount the pictures you have found on the card stock paper using the glue or glue sticks.
* Cut around the picture leaving an edge of card stock showing as a frame.
* Hang the pictures in various places on the classroom walls using an approved mounting material.

What to Do

1. Listen to the children and notice if they comment on the pictures and if they engage each other or adults in conversation about the pictures. Notice if they ask questions about the pictures and seek out more information as to why they are on display.

2. Ask the children questions to encourage them to continue to explore what the pictures might mean and why they are on display. You might say, *Yes, that is a picture of a stack of sticks. Can you think of any other time you've seen or heard of a stack of sticks?*

3. Provide more clues, either visually or verbally, to children who need them but avoid directly mentioning the story. The idea is to get the children thinking, exploring, and engaging each other in conversation.

4. When you are ready and you think the children are ready, tell or read the story.

Reviewing What the Children Learned

* After a day of fun and discovery about the day's story, use the clue cards to prompt individual children to remember specific elements of the story. For example, you might show a child a picture of blonde hair and say, *This hair reminds me of something we talked about today. Does it remind you of anything?*

More to Do

* After telling the story, move the Story Clues to the Story Wall (see page 22) so the children can use them as props for retelling and reinventing the day's story.
* Add props to the Dramatic Play Center that the children can use to retell the day's story.
* Tell the story again. Stop occasionally to ask the children what they could change about the story, and then incorporate these ideas into the story to change it into something entirely new. For example, when retelling the story of the "Three Little Pigs," stop and ask the children how they might change the part when the three pigs decided to leave home to make their own way in the world. *What would have happened if one of the pigs had decided to keep on living at home with his mother?* Or, consider asking if they would change anything about the part of the story where the wolf is knocking on the door of the first pig's house. *What would happen if the pig opened the door and invited the wolf inside?*

Related Books

Select books that are related to the topic of the story. For example, if your story is "Goldilocks and the Three Bears," then you would provide other books about adventurous little girls, or about bears. Relating different elements of your classroom to the topic of the story enhances the children's overall learning and encourages them to make connections.

Story Trip

What the Children Will Learn

✖ To be curious about story time
✖ To retell story elements in sequence

Materials

glue
Mod Podge® or other sealant (adult use only)
old maps
spray paint in two or three colors (adult use only)
suitcase (old or new)

Preparation

✖ Make sure the suitcase is empty and clean.
✖ When the children are not in the classroom, paint the suitcase in a colorful pattern using the spray paints (adult use only step).
✖ Cut up the old maps and glue pieces to the sides of the suitcase.
✖ Use Mod Podge or another sealant (adult use only step) to cover the map cutouts. Several coats may be required.
✖ Allow the suitcase to dry thoroughly.
✖ Fill the suitcase with items that will be used to tell a story.

What to Do

1. At the beginning of story time, recite this rhyme to draw the children's attention to the suitcase. Remember to add your own personality and body movements to make things interesting.

   Get out the suitcase and pack your things.
   We're going to take a trip and fly with wings.

Going on a road trip, going to ride a train,
Hop on a bus or fly in a plane.

We're going to take a trip and fly with wings.
We've packed our bags with lots of things.

2. After gaining the children's attention, open the suitcase and begin to tell a story using the props inside.

Reviewing What the Children Learned

Ask individual children the following questions:
* *What did we find in the suitcase today?*
* *What do you remember about this (show an item from suitcase)?*
* *What happened at the beginning (middle, end) of our story today?*

More to Do

* Put a map in the suitcase and sing this song to the tune of "Here We Go 'Round the Mulberry Bush" as you bring the suitcase out, prepare to look at it, and take an imaginary trip.

  Packing a bag to take a trip, take a trip, take a trip.
  Packing a bag to take a trip across _____
  (USA or any other destination).

* Invite the children to bring things from home and put them in the suitcase. When you open the suitcase, the children can tell about the items. This promotes language development and self-confidence as the children speak in front of their peers. Ask the children to name some places they have been and tell a short story about each. Create a chart to show the different places, or hang up a map and mark the locations on the map.
* Fold a piece of paper in half and seal two edges, leaving one long edge open for the top. Add a U-shaped handle and decorate the paper to make your own suitcase. Cut out

Story Play: Building Language and Literacy One Story at a Time

magazine pictures of the things you would pack to take on a trip and fill the suitcase with the pictures. Encourage the children to tell the story of their imaginary trip. This could lead to making a simple construction paper book of the story, with a few words and pictures. This book could go into the child's Story Bag (see page 23) to share at home.

✖ If possible, provide duplicate items of the ones in the story suitcase and send one home with each child. Ask the children to tell that day's story at home, using the suitcase item as a prop.

Related Books

Ella's Trip to the Museum by Elaine Clayton

Eloise's Summer Vacation by Kay Thompson, Lisa McClatchy, and Tammie Lyon

I'm Going to Grandma's by Mary Ann Hoberman

It's Vacation Time by Lerryn Korda

My Trip to Grandma's by Emma Less

Round Trip by Ann Jonas

Strega Nona Takes a Vacation by Tomie dePaola

Stringbean's Trip to the Shining Sea by Vera B. and Jennifer Williams

Taking Stories Outside

The Story Tree

What the Children Will Learn

✖ To connect the stories they hear with the natural world
✖ To explore nature through stories

Materials

real tree that is in an accessible, safe area
props and materials for a story

Preparation

✖ Gather the materials you will need for the story you intend to tell. Since this activity will take place outside, prepare a story that has an outdoor theme. The Story Tree setting will be especially effective if you choose a story involving trees or the familiar creatures that live and find shelter in them, like squirrels and robins. See the list of related books, on page 45.
✖ Place a blanket or a Story Sheet (see page 28) near the base of the tree.

What to Do

1. Once outside, place your materials near the tree so you can reach them easily when needed.
2. Stand behind the tree and chant the following:

Hey, hey, hey,
Look at me!
I'm the giant (little,
wide, skinny) story tree!

Listen to my tale, one and all,
As I spin my yarn big and tall.

3. Say, "Today we will share a story about _________________" as you come out from behind the tree and begin your storytelling experience.

Reviewing What the Children Learned

- Ask individual children to recall elements of the story you told.

More to Do

- Create a storytelling tree in the classroom by adding a potted tree to the room.
- Have the children collect leaves and small twigs that have fallen from the Story Tree. Use these and other art materials to help the children create their own Story Tree collage on heavy paper.
- To encourage conversation and exploration, put an assortment of books, both fiction and non-fiction, about trees and woodland animals in the Story Corner (see page 27).

Related Books

The Great Kapok Tree by Lynne Cherry

The Magician and McTree by Patricia Coombs

Our Tree Named Steve by Alan Zweibel and David Catrow

The Tale of Squirrel Nutkin by Beatrix Potter

A Tree Is Nice by Janice May Udry

Garden Stories

What the Children Will Learn

- About different kinds of gardens
- To connect the stories they hear with the natural world

Materials

blanket or story sheet
class garden that is in a safe and accessible place
materials needed for any story you choose to tell

Preparation

- Gather the materials you will need to tell the story you have chosen. Because this activity will take place in the garden, tell a story that features plants, vegetables, flowers, worms, bees, butterflies, or any other garden-connected character. Consider telling "The Old Man Who Made Flowers Bloom" by Seki, which is a Japanese folktale about a garden. "Mary, Mary, Quite Contrary" is a common nursery rhyme about gardens, and the book *The Summer My Father Was Ten* by Pat Brisson is a story of a father who passes the tradition of gardening down to his daughter.
- If you do not have a class garden, maybe a teacher or caregiver would be willing to host the group for storytelling in his garden. Or perhaps your area has a public park with a garden where you could take the class.

What to Do

1. Take the children to the garden, spread out a blanket or story sheet, and settle in for a great storytelling experience.
2. After the story is over, talk about the real garden. Do you see flowers? Do you see vegetables? Is it like the garden in the story? How is it the same? How is it different? Encourage conversation and observation.

Reviewing What the Children Learned

✖ Ask individual children to recall elements of the story you told.

✖ Talk with the children about what grows in the garden they saw.

More to Do

✖ Create a mini-garden in your classroom in small plastic tubs. Add some hardy, non-toxic houseplants. You can also fill a small tub with sand and add plastic garden play pieces for a fun and satisfying play experience.

✖ Plant some items in the class garden that are connected with familiar stories. Consider planting beans to go along with "Jack and the Beanstalk" or flowers for the telling of "The Secret Garden."

✖ If any of the children in your class help with gardening at home, encourage them to talk about it and tell their own stories.

✖ Add some small plastic or ceramic animals or insects to the indoor garden to enhance the telling of books like *The Wide Mouthed Frog* or *The Very Quiet Cricket*.

Related Books

Eating the Alphabet: Fruits and Vegetables from A to Z by Lois Ehlert

Flower Garden by Eve Bunting

Growing Vegetable Soup by Lois Ehlert

Jack's Garden by Henry Cole

My Garden by Kevin Henkes

Potato Joe by Keith Baker

Pumpkin Circle: The Story of a Garden by George Levenson

The Runaway Garden: A Delicious Story That's Good for You, Too! by Jeffery Schatzer

Seed, Sprout, Pumpkin, Pie by Jill Esbaum

The Talking Vegetables by Won-Ldy Paye

Tops & Bottoms by Janet Stevens

Vegetable Garden by Douglas Florian

Playhouse Stories

What the Children Will Learn

✳ To connect the stories they hear with their home environment

Materials

basket (optional)
blanket or story sheet
material for any story you choose to tell
playground playhouse in a safe and accessible place

Preparation

✳ Gather the materials you will need for the story you will tell. Since this activity will take place in the playhouse, consider a story about houses or families such as the books *Feast for 10* by Cathryn Falwell, *The Doorbell Rang* by Pat Hutchins, and *Silly Lilly and the Four Seasons* by Agnes Rosenstiehl or the classic poem, story, or a version of "This Is the House That Jack Built," such as the one by Simms Taback.

What to Do

1. Once outside, join the children who are playing in or near the playhouse. Spread out a plastic tablecloth, blanket, or story sheet (see page 28) for comfortable seating, and invite the children to join you.
   Hint: Consider decorating an old basket and using it for all your outside storytelling. Fill the basket with outdoor puppets and props.

2. Begin your story. Be ready for all the children to want to join in as soon as they discover what is happening, so make sure you have lots of room.

Reviewing What the Children Learned

- Ask individual children to recall elements of the story.
- Ask individual children to retell the story using the props and materials you used to tell the story.

More to Do

- The Dramatic Play Center is the perfect place to encourage the children to recall story elements and retell stories in their own words. Change the materials in the Dramatic Play Center so they reflect stories that you are telling or that the children know.
- After telling a playhouse story such as "This Is the House That Jack Built," provide art materials such as craft sticks, heavy card stock paper, and glue and encourage the children to create their own house collage. Label each one "This Is the House That [child's name] Built."

Related Books

All Kinds of Families! by Mary Ann Hoberman
Anno's Counting House by Mitsumasa Anno
Diary of a Worm by Doreen Cronin
The House from Morning to Night by Daniele Bour

Fishing Boat

Materials

fisherman's boots
large bucket
paddles
paint
paintbrushes
slickers or raincoats
small fishing boat such as a canoe or flat-bottomed boat
straw hat or fisherman's hats

Preparation

✖ Place the boat on the playground.
✖ Let the children help paint the boat (with careful supervision) or invite parent volunteers to paint the boat.
✖ Put the paddles in the boat to represent oars.
✖ Put the storytelling props (hats, slickers, and boots) in the large bucket and place it near the boat.

What to Do

1. Encourage the children to play in and around the boat. You may want to keep a tape recorder or pad and paper on hand to record the many stories that they will naturally develop as they play.
2. Pretend to row the boat while you sing "Row, Row, Row Your Boat." Sing the song fast, slowly, and at many different speeds,

changing the word *gently* in the song to other words like *quietly*, *swiftly*, and other appropriate words.

Reviewing What the Children Learned

Remember that this is an open-ended, child-directed storytelling experience.

✻ Ask the children open-ended questions that relate to the stories they are creating. Your questions should always encourage the children to think more deeply about the things they are doing and to take the story further if they are interested.

More to Do

✻ Consider learning and retelling one of the child-developed stories during a more formal storytelling session. The children will be delighted, and so will you.

✻ Place a small tub, some magnetic alphabet letters, and two or three magnetic fishing poles in a corner of the classroom. Encourage the children to fish for and identify the letters. Think about other things you can use in the fishing pool.

✻ A discussion of the artist Claude Monet and his well-known water lily paintings can easily be extended into the outdoors, with the boat as inspiration. Add a straw hat to the collection of props. Place a small easel in the boat along with a palette of paints and encourage the children to paint their own stories. Take pictures of the children and display them on a blue bulletin board filled with pictures of water lilies.

Related Books

Boats: Speeding! Sailing! Cruising! by Patricia Hubbell
How to Be a Pirate by John Malam
Row, Row, Row Your Boat by Heather Collins
Stanley Goes Fishing by Craig Frazier
Ste-e-e-eamboat a-Comin' by Jill Esbaum
Who Sank the Boat? by Pamela Allen

Nursery Rhyme Story Time

CHAPTER 4

Two Little Blackbirds

What the Children Will Learn

* To identify at least five colors
* To listen for rhythm and rhyme

Materials

bird pattern (see page 153)
clear tape
craft paper
scissors (adult use only)

Preparation

* Cut out enough birds so that you have two for each child. Color them with crayons or markers. You will need two of each color.
* Cut ½" × 3" bands from the craft paper. You will need one for each bird puppet.
* Form the bands into a ring shape and tape securely. Size the band to fit snugly on the top of a child's index finger, like a finger puppet.

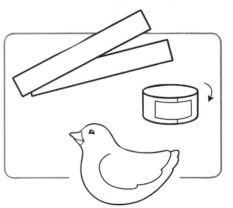

53

✹ Create bird finger puppets by taping a band to the back of each bird illustration.

What to Do

1. Invite the children to choose a bird color and place one bird on each index finger. Make sure you have enough bird puppets for the number of children in the group. Each child will need a matching set of birds.

2. As you recite this familiar nursery rhyme, the children respond when they hear the color of the bird puppet they are holding.

Two Little Blackbirds

Two little blackbirds
   (yellow, green, red, blue)
Sitting on a hill.
One named Jack.
One named Jill.

3. After each name (Jack, Jill), pause as you wait for the children holding the color of the bird mentioned to respond by holding up their bird puppets in turn.

   Fly away, Jack.
   Fly away, Jill.

4. Again, pause after each name to give the children time to respond.

   Come back, Jack.
   Come back, Jill.

5. Pause again after each name to allow for response.
6. Repeat the poem until all the colors have been mentioned and all the children have had a chance to participate.

✳ Ask individual children the following questions:
   What color are the birds you are holding?
   What color birds did we talk about in our poem?

More to Do

✳ Write the name of the color on the band of each finger puppet, so the children can begin to recognize the color words.

✳ Provide magazines with bird pictures and have the children create a colorful bird collage.

✳ Place one of each pair of bird puppets on a table, cover with a cloth, and quietly remove one bird. Remove the cloth and have the children tell which bird is missing.

✳ Repeat the activity using different animals (monkeys, bears, dogs, cats), with or without finger puppets. For example:

   Two little monkeys sitting on a hill . . .

✳ Instead of the names in the poem, use the children's names and create a matching rhyme to use in place of the traditional one. For example, if John were holding a blue bird, your poem would be:

   Two little blue birds
   Sitting on the lawn.
   One named Jack.
   One named John.
   Fly away, Jack.
   Fly away, John.
   Come back, Jack.
   Come back, John.

Related Books

Are You My Mother? by P.D. Eastman
Birds by Kevin Henkes
Flap Your Wings by P. D. Eastman
My Nest Is Best by P.D. Eastman

Jack Be Nimble

What the Children Will Learn

✖ To develop fine and gross motor skills
✖ To understand what the word *half* means
✖ Some new words to describe movement

Materials

child-safe scissors
red, yellow, and orange craft paper
tape
two small paper plates for each child

Preparation

✖ Cut the red, yellow, and orange craft paper to look like candle flames.

What to Do

1. Tell the rhyme "Jack Be Nimble" to the children. Repeat it several times, inviting the children to say it with you.

   ### Jack Be Nimble
   Jack be nimble.
   Jack be quick.
   Jack jump over the candlestick.

2. After introducing the rhyme, invite the children to join you in the Art Center where they can each make their own candlestick.

3. Give each child two small paper plates. Have them roll one plate tightly and tape it.

4. Help the children cut across the rolled plate to cut off about an inch. The remainder of the rolled plate becomes the candle.

5. Have the children fold the other plate in half and then in half again. Cut the folded plate 1" in from the point and cut a 1" slit on each side of the middle cut. Unfold it. The candle will be inserted from the bottom (see illustration).

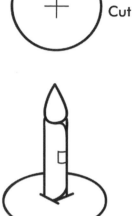

6. Insert the candle through the opening in the second plate and tape it in place.

7. Help the children tape or staple the flames to the top of the candle.

8. Write the rhyme for every child, inserting the child's name in the rhyme.

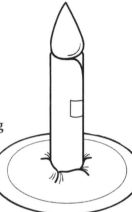

[Child's name] Be Nimble

[child's name] be nimble.
[child's name] be quick.
[child's name] jump over the candlestick.

9. Attach the poem to each child's candlestick and send the candlesticks home with the children along with a note asking the parents to have the children retell the rhyme at home. The family can change the name in the rhyme to a sister, brother, daddy, mama, granny, or any other family member.

Reviewing What the Children Learned

✖ Are the children able to repeat the rhyme?
✖ Are the children able to manipulate the tape and scissors to create the candlestick?
✖ Ask individual children the following questions (see the "More to Do" section):
  When we say Jack is nimble, *what does that mean?*
  Quick *is a word that tells us how Jack moved. What are other words that describe how people might move?*

More to Do

✖ Create some flame-inspired artwork by dipping marbles in red, yellow, and orange paint and rolling them around in a shallow tray into which you have placed colorful art paper.

✖ Using a real candlestick and an unlit candle, play this fun and physical game. Place the candlestick on the floor in an area where it is safe for the children to jump. Have the children take turns saying the rhyme and jumping over the candlestick. Replace the name Jack with the name of the child jumping.

✖ Jack in the rhyme was *nimble* and *quick*. Talk about other words that describe how people move. Ask the children what other words they could use to change the story of Jack and the candlestick. Bring out the candlestick and unlit candle and have the children move over the candle in the ways they mentioned. Can they move slowly, fast, or by hopping? Can they hop on one foot, two feet?

Related Books

Bridget's Book of Nursery Rhymes by Bridget Strevens-Marzo
Favorite Nursery Rhymes from Mother Goose by Scott Gustafson
Fox Be Nimble by James Marshall

Humpty Dumpty

What the Children Will Learn

* That something that is whole can be divided into parts
* To recognize rhyming words

Materials

Band-Aids™
markers
one large piece of red poster board
Storyboard (see page 21)
two large pieces of white poster board
Velcro™ hook tape

Preparation

* Cut the red poster board in half and use the markers to draw lines to make it look like a brick wall. Print the names of the children in the classroom on the bricks.
* Cut a large oval from one piece of white poster board and create a face on it using the markers.
* Cut another large oval from white poster board, create a similar face, and add lots of cracks.
* Put Velcro hook tape on the backs of the pieces.

Josie	Anne	Juan	Grace
	Mya	Kate	Luke	R.J.
Matt	Aiden	Jai	Harley

What to Do

1. Gather the children around a Storyboard and use the following rhyme to tell the children the story of Humpty Dumpty using the props you made.

   Humpty Dumpty
   Humpty Dumpty sat on a wall
   Humpty Dumpty had a great fall
   All the king's horses and all the king's men
   Couldn't put Humpty together again

2. When you are finished with the story, have each child choose a Band-Aid and use a permanent marker to print her name on it (offer help as needed).

3. Have the children put their Band-Aids on the cracked egg to help put it "together again."

Reviewing What the Children Learned

Ask individual children the following questions:
* *What happened to Humpty Dumpty in the poem?*
* *Why do you think Humpty Dumpty was sitting on the wall?*
* *Have you ever worn a Band-Aid? Why did you need it?*

More to Do

* Use the same materials to make a smaller version of this story to send home with the children, along with a note explaining the activity and asking that the children retell the story to the adults at home.
* Ask families to save very well-washed eggshells and send them in with their children. Before using them for this activity, sanitize them by soaking them for 10 minutes in a diluted bleach solution (1 tablespoon of bleach to 1 quart of water, or ¼ cup of bleach to a gallon of water). Let them dry completely before proceeding with the activity. Crush the eggshells by

placing them in a zippered bag and using a rolling pin. Put these crushed shells in the Art Center along with egg-shaped cutouts. Encourage the children to create a Humpty Dumpty Eggshell Collage. You can also color crushed eggshells by placing them in a zippered bag along with some food coloring and a drop of rubbing alcohol. Zip the bag shut and shake, shake, shake until all the eggshell pieces are covered with color. Spread on paper towels to dry.

Note: Eggshells must be completely dry before gluing.

✳ Create a Humpty Dumpty puzzle using a large piece of poster board. Draw Humpty Dumpty on the poster board and cut into puzzle-shaped pieces. Ask the children to help you put Humpty Dumpty back together again.

Related Books

And the Dish Ran Away with the Spoon by Janet Stevens and Susan Stevens Crummel

The Big, Big Wall by Reginald Howard

Dimity Dumpty: The Story of Humpty's Little Sister by Bob Graham

Humpty Dumpty by Etienne Delessert

Humpty Dumpty by W. W. Denslow

Humpty Dumpty Climbs Again by Dave Horowitz

What REALLY Happened to Humpty? by Jeanie Franz Ransom

Hickety Pickety

What the Children Will Learn

* To correctly order the numbers one through seven
* To recognize the numerals 1 though 7

Materials

glue

hen pattern (see page 154)

laminating machine or clear contact paper

markers

nest pattern (see page 155)

scissors (adult use only)

Storyboard (see page 21)

Velcro™ hook-and-loop tape

Preparation

* Duplicate the hen pattern on page 154 seven times.
* Copy the nest pattern on pages 155 seven times.
* Use the markers to color each hen a different color (black, red, orange, yellow, green, blue, and purple).
* Print a numeral (1 through 7) on each hen.
* Draw one egg in the first nest, two in the second; continue with all seven nests.
* Use the markers to color the nests. Match the color of the nest to the color of the matching hen. If you printed the number 1 on the red hen, then add some red color to the nest with one egg in it. Do not color the whole nest the matching color; just add some color for highlighting.
* Laminate the hens and nests. Add the Velcro hook tape to the back of each item.

What to Do

1. Teach the children the following rhyme during story time, using the pieces you have created. Pass the hens out to the children and say the rhyme several times, changing the color each time. Have the children come up to the Storyboard and match their hens to the nests with the correct number of eggs and color. Notice that the second time you say the rhyme, you change the word *gentlemen* to *children*.
2. Repeat this activity until all the children have had a turn to match.

Hickety Pickety

Hickety, pickety, my black hen,
She lays eggs for the gentlemen.
Gentlemen come every day
To see what my black hen did lay.

Hickety, pickety, my ________ hen
She lays eggs for all the children.
Children come every day
To see what my _______ hen did lay.

Reviewing What the Children Learned

- Ask individual children to place the hens in the correct numerical order.

More to Do

- Add a chicken puppet to the Dramatic Play Center. Suggest that the children find materials with which they can build the hen a nest. Add plastic eggs and watch the children's imaginations take flight.

  Hint: You can create a nest by using the bottom of a plastic jug, such as for water, milk, or juice. Cut off the top of the jug and fill it with nesting material.

✖ This is a great story for a Pizza Story Box. Use different colored chickens and eggs. Add a nest pattern and place all the items in a Pizza Story Box. Encourage the children to revisit the rhyme with these new materials.

✖ Using plastic eggs, challenge the children to solve simple addition and subtraction problems.

Related Books

The Chicken Sisters by Laura Numeroff

Chicken Soup by Jean Van Leeuwen

Louise, The Adventures of a Chicken by Kate DiCamillo

My Life as a Chicken by Ellen A. Kelley

My Painted House, My Friendly Chicken, and Me by Maya Angelou

The Painter Who Loved Chickens by Olivier Dunrea

The Problem with Chickens by Bruce McMillan

Silly Chicken by Rukhsana Khan

Six Chicks by Henrietta Branford

Little Boy Blue

What the Children Will Learn

- About music, sounds, and instruments

Materials

chopstick, dowel rod, or unsharpened pencil (for the "maestro wand")
musical instruments (horn, guitar, banjo, spoons, kazoo, fiddle), or pictures of instruments
Storyboard (see page 21)

Preparation

- If using pictures of musical instruments, cut out the pictures and laminate them.

What to Do

1. As you chant the following poem, show the musical instrument for each verse or place the picture of each instrument on the Storyboard as you say each verse.

Little Boy Blue
Little Boy Blue, come play your horn,
The sheep's in the meadow, and
The cow's in the corn.

Little Boy Blue, come play your guitar,
The horse and the mule are grazing afar.

Little Boy Blue, come play your banjo,
The chickens in the barnyard do-si-do.

Little Boy Blue, come play the spoons,
The cat and the cow just jumped over the moon.

Little Boy Blue, come play your kazoo,
The roosters say cock-a-doodle-doo.

Little Boy Blue, wave your maestro wand,
Conduct the ducks swimming on the pond.

Little Boy Blue, come play your fiddle,
All the animals sing hey diddle-diddle.

Hey Diddle-diddle-diddle-diddle-diddle-diddle!

2. Chant the poem again as you and the children march around the room, acting out how to play each instrument.

Reviewing What the Children Learned

✷ Ask individual children to name the musical instruments.

More to Do

✷ If you know other teachers or have family members who play musical instruments, invite them to the classroom for an instrument "petting zoo."
✷ Add toy instruments to the Dramatic Play Center.
✷ Listen to the CD, *Getting Loose with Mother Goose and Some of Her Silly Friends*, and sing along playing each imaginary instrument.

Related Books

Charlie Parker Played Be Bop by Christopher Raschka
Humpty Dumpty and Other Rhymes by Iona Opie
Little Boy Blue by Josie Stewart and Lynn Salem
Music, Music for Everyone by Vera Williams
Zin! Zin! Zin! A Violin by Lloyd Moss and Marjorie Priceman

Songs, Poems, Chants, and Fingerplays

Rooster Call

What the Children Will Learn

* To listen for the rhymes
* About the sound a rooster makes
* Fine motor skills: scissors and glue

Materials

clear tape

card stock paper or 5" × 8" index cards

copies of the rooster pattern (see page 156)

craft sticks

crayons or markers

glue sticks

child-safe scissors

Preparation

* Copy the rooster pattern on page 156. You will need one rooster for each child.

What to Do

1. Tell the children the following rooster chant. When you come to the line "Cock-a-doodle-doo," encourage the children to chant along with you.

   Rooster Call
   Cock-a-doodle-doo
   There is a rooster calling you!

   Cock-a-doodle-doo
   Do you hear him too?

   Cock-a-doodle-doo
   The morning sun is bright.

   Cock-a-doodle-doo
   Everything is all right.

   Cock-a-doodle
   Cock-a-doodle
   Cock-a-doodle-doo!

2. Give the children the rooster patterns. Encourage them to color their roosters with the crayons or markers.
3. Let the children cut out their roosters. Offer help where needed.
4. To make the roosters sturdy, have the children glue their rooster cutouts to card stock, then cut around them again. Glue or tape each rooster to a craft stick.
5. Say the chant together while the children use their roosters to act it out.
6. Add new verses, and encourage the children to supply the rhymes.

Reviewing What the Children Learned

✷ Are the children able to use the scissors and glue to make their own stick puppets?
✷ Ask individual children the following question: *Why do roosters crow?*

More to Do

✱ Have the children search through nature or feed supply magazines to find pictures of roosters. They can cut them out and make a rooster collage.

✱ Copy the pattern on page 156 six times or more, and use the pieces to create a patterning game. Color each pair of roosters a different color. For example, you could color two roosters red, two yellow, and two green. Place the roosters in the Math Center. Begin a pattern such as red rooster, yellow rooster, and challenge the children to continue it.

✱ When transitioning from one activity to another, such as when you are preparing to go outside, call to them using the following Rooster Call chant.

Rooster Call Transition Time Chant

Cock-a-doodle-doo

There's a teacher calling you!

Cock-a-doodle-doo

Do you hear me too?

Cock-a-doodle-doo

We're having such a good day.

Cock-a-doodle-doo

Let's go outside to play.

Related Books

Brewster the Rooster by Devin Scillian

Cook-a-Doodle-Doo! by Janet Stevens and
   Susan Stevens Crummel

The King's Chorus by Linda Hayward

The Mixed-Up Rooster by Pamela Duncan Edwards

Rooster's Off to See the World by Eric Carle

Gator Hunt

What the Children Will Learn

✻ To develop their imaginations
✻ To remember the sequence of motions in the chant

Materials

backpack pattern (see page 157)
erasable markers
laminating machine or clear contact paper
markers

Preparation

✻ Enlarge the backpack pattern on page 157. You will need one copy.
✻ Make multiple copies of the backpack pattern on page 157 without enlarging it. You will need one for each child.
✻ Cut out the large backpack. Use the markers to color it, then laminate it.

What to Do

1. At story time, show the large laminated backpack and ask the children if they would like to go on a story adventure with you. Be dramatic. Suggest that the adventure might be dangerous and they should think hard about whether or not they want to go.
2. When the children agree to go, tell them you are going to take them on a Gator Hunt! Ask them what they might need to bring.
3. Use the erasable marker to write the items the children mention on the backpack. Be sure a flashlight is included.

4. Tell the children that they will be going in a boat to hunt gators with you. Pretend to hand out life vests and encourage the children to pretend to put them on. Remember to wear one yourself.

5. Begin the gator hunt chant. The children should repeat each line after you. (The children's lines are italicized in the chant. This is called a "call back.") It is helpful to have another teacher sit with the children and lead them in their part until they are familiar with how this type of story works.

6. Be dramatic as you tell this story, and use large body movements to act out the scene. Row the boat, shade your eyes with your hands when looking around, put your finger to your lips, and shush the children when you are talking about being quiet.

7. When it is time to get in the boat, demonstrate by standing up, pretending to climb into a boat, and settling yourself on the boat seat. Ask the children to do the same.

8. When you are leading the children in the parts of the chant where everyone is walking, slap your thighs alternately to imitate a walking rhythm. This will keep the children focused.

9. When the children know the chant, have them add the motions that are described in parentheses. Remember to relax and have fun!

10. When you lead the children in the last section of the chant, where you are running from the gator, begin to slap your thighs quickly to imitate the sound of running, and remember to go through each motion again.

Going on a Gator Hunt

(begin to slap your thighs in a walking rhythm)
Going on a gator hunt.
Going on a gator hunt.
Going to find a gator. (shade eyes with hand)
Going to find a gator.

A long green gator (stretch out arms to indicate length)
A long green gator
With big yellow eyes (circle your eyes with your fingers)
With big yellow eyes
And a swishing tail. (stand up quickly, put one hand behind
   you, and swish it)
And a swishing tail.

Climb in your boat. (pretend to climb in)
Climb in your boat.
Quiet while we float. (finger to lips in a shushing motion)
Quiet while we float. (whisper this line until you have reached
   the other side of the swamp, then pretend to get out of
   the boat)

(begin to slap thighs)
Going on a gator hunt.
Going on a gator hunt.
Going to find a gator (shade eyes with hand).
Going to find a gator.

A long green gator (stretch out arms to indicate length)
A long green gator
With big yellow eyes (circle your eyes with your fingers)
With big yellow eyes
And a swishing tail. (stand up quickly, put one hand behind
   you, and swish it)
And a swishing tail.

Oh look, (shade eyes with hand)
Oh look,
Over there! (point in any direction with the other hand)
Over there!
It's a river bank.
It's a river bank.
Climb out of the boat.
Climb out of the boat.

Can't go over it. (wave one arm high in front of yourself)
Can't go over it.
Can't go under it. (swoop the same arm down low)
Can't go under it.
Can't go around it. (shrug shoulders)
Can't go around it.
We'll have to go across it. (nod head firmly)
We'll have to go across it.

(begin to slap thighs)
Going on a gator hunt.
Going on a gator hunt.
Going to find a gator. (shade eyes with hand)
Going to find a gator.

A long green gator (stretch out arms to indicate length)
A long green gator
With big yellow eyes (circle your eyes with your fingers)
With big yellow eyes
And a swishing tail. (stand up quickly, put one hand behind
   you, and swish it)
And a swishing tail.

Oh look, (shade eyes with hand)
Oh look,
Over there! (point in any direction with the other hand)
Over there!
It's a bridge.
It's a bridge.
A swinging bridge. (swing both hands in front of yourself)
A swinging bridge.

Can't go over it. (wave one arm high in front of yourself)
Can't go over it.
Can't go under it. (swoop the same arm down low)
Can't go under it.
Can't go around it. (shrug shoulders)
Can't go around it.
We'll have to go across it. (nod head firmly)
We'll have to go across it.

(stand up and pretend to hold the sides of the swinging
    bridge as you lead the children across; remember to sway
    from side to side as you walk in place)
Swing step, swing step, swing, step.
Swing step, swing step, swing, step.

Going on a gator hunt. (slap thighs)
Going on a gator hunt.
Going to find a gator. (shade eyes with hand)
Going to find a gator.

A long green gator (stretch out arms to indicate length)
A long green gator
With big yellow eyes (circle eyes with fingers)
With big yellow eyes
And a swishing tail. (stand up quickly, put one hand behind
    you and swish it)
And a swishing tail.

Oh look, (shade eyes with hand)
Oh look,
Over there! (point with other hand)
Over there!
It's a river.
It's a river.
A muddy river.
A muddy river.

Can't go over it. (wave one arm high in front of yourself)
Can't go over it.
Can't go under it. (swoop the same arm down low)
Can't go under it.
Can't go around it. (shrug shoulders)
Can't go around it.
We'll have to swim across it. (nod head firmly)
We'll have to swim across it.

(make large swimming motions)
Swim, swim, swim.
Swim, swim, swim.

Going on a gator hunt. (slap thighs)
Going on a gator hunt.
Going to find a gator. (shade eyes with hand)
Going to find a gator.

A long green gator (stretch out arms to indicate length)
A long green gator
With big yellow eyes (circle eyes with fingers)
With big yellow eyes
And a swishing tail. (stand up quickly, put one hand behind
   you and swish it)
And a swishing tail.

Oh look, (shade eyes with hand)
Oh look,
Over there! (point with other hand)
Over there!
It's a swamp.
It's a swamp.
A marshy swamp.
A marshy swamp.

Can't go over it. (wave one arm high in front of yourself)
Can't go over it.
Can't go under it. (swoop the same arm down low)
Can't go under it.
Can't go around it. (shrug shoulders)
Can't go around it.
We'll have to tiptoe across it. (nod head firmly)
We'll have to tiptoe across it.

(lead the children in tiptoeing in place)
Tiptoe, tiptoe, tiptoe.
Tiptoe, tiptoe, tiptoe.

Oh look, (stop tiptoeing and shade eyes with hand)
Oh look,
Over there! (point with other hand)
Over there!
It's something green! (look excitedly in the direction you are
    pointing)
It's something green!
Looks kind of strange. (make a quizzical expression)
Looks kind of strange.

Shhhhhhhhhhhhhhhhhhh! (finger to lips)
Shhhhhhhhhhhhhhhhhhh!

(reach out and pretend to be feeling something that is in front
of you)

It feels rough and crackly. (use an excited tone as you continue
to *feel* something in front of you)

It feels rough and crackly.

What could it be? (look at the children with a quizzical
expression and widened eyes)

What could it be?

(at this point in the chant, the children stop repeating what you
say and participate with you as you tell them what to do)

It's too dark to tell.

Take off your backpack. (pretend to shrug off backpacks)

Get out your flashlights. (pretend to rummage in backpack
for a flashlight; pretend to draw the flashlight out of the
backpack and point it in front of yourself)

When I count to three, turn on the flashlight.

SHHHHHHH! (finger of other hand to lips)

One, two, three . . . CLICK. (make a motion as if turning
on a flashlight)

Yi-i-i-i-i-kes-s-s-s-s-s-s-s!
  (look frightened)

It's a gator . . . R-U-U-UN-N-N-N!
  (slap thighs quickly)

Tiptoe, tiptoe, tiptoe. (lead
  children in tiptoeing in place)

R-U-U-UN-N-N-N! (slap thighs)

Swim, swim, swim. (lead children in swimming in place)

R-U-U-UN-N-N-N! (slap thighs)

Swing step, swing step, swing step. (lead children in running
  in place as they sway from side to side)

R-U-U-UN-N-N-N! (slap thighs)

Jump in the boat (pretend to climb in)

And row across the swamp. (pretend to row)

Quiet so the swamp gators won't know what direction we are going. (finger to lips)

Dock the boat, jump out, and (pretend to climb out)

R-U-U-UN-N-N-N for home! (slap thighs)

Shut the door. (pretend to shut a door behind yourself)

Wow, safe at last! (wipe forehead with hand in a gesture of relief)

Oh no! (pretend to look around for something)

We forgot something . . . (spread out empty hands)

Our backpacks!

Do you want to go back and get your backpack? (look quizzically at the children)

Not me! (firmly shake head to indicate no and tap yourself on your chest with your index finger)

11. After the chant, give each child an individual-sized copy of the backpack pattern. Let them take it to the Art Center and use the materials there to color and decorate it.

12. Ask the children to tell you what they would pack in their backpack if they were going on a great adventure. Write the names of those items on their backpacks. Alternatively, they could draw them or cut out pictures from magazines and glue them to the backpack pattern.

Reviewing What the Children Learned

Ask individual children the following questions:

✱ *What was the first thing we came across on our adventure? The second? The third?*

✱ *What did we put in our backpack to take with us?*

✱ *Were you scared?*

Story Play: Building Language and Literacy One Story at a Time

More to Do

✱ Add a couple of real backpacks to the Dramatic Play Center so the children can pack them and pretend to go on another great adventure.

✱ Add a gator puppet and other animals (bear, lion, and so on) that they could use to go on a hunt.

✱ Send a copy of the chant home along with each child. Include a note asking families to use the chant to tell the story with their child.

Related Books

The Cajun Cornbread Boy by Dianne De Las Casas
Gator Gumbo: A Spicy-Hot Tale by Candace Fleming
Izzie Lizzie Alligator: A Tale of a Big Lizard by Suzanne Tate
There's an Alligator Under My Bed by Mercer Mayer

Five Little Apples

What the Children Will Learn

✖ To count backwards from five to one
✖ To begin to think about the concept of pollination

Materials

apple pattern (see page 158)
bee pattern (see page 158)
laminating machine or clear contact paper
markers
Storyboard (see page 21) or Storytelling Apron (see page 24)
tree pattern (see page 158)
Velcro™ hook tape

Preparation

✖ Make five copies of the apple pattern on page 158.
✖ Make one copy of the bee pattern on page 158.
✖ Make one copy of the tree pattern on page 158.
✖ Color the apples with the markers. Be creative! Apples are not just red, and even red apples might have shades of other colors. Color the bee and the tree.
✖ Laminate the pieces for durability.
✖ Attach a piece of Velcro tape to the back of each piece.

What to Do

1. Use the Storyboard or the Storytelling Apron and the poem to tell the story of the Five Little Apples. First, place the tree and all five apples on the board or apron. Keep the bee hidden for now.

2. Remove one apple with each verse. The first time you tell the story, resist the temptation to get the children to count how many apples are left. When they are more familiar with the

story, you can ask them to help you and before long, they will be counting them naturally.

3. When you reach the last line and all of the apples are gone, place the bee on the board near the tree.

Five Little Apples

Five little apples hanging on a tree,
You can pick one, they are free.

Four little apples hanging on a tree,
The wind blew hard, now there are three.

Three little apples hanging on a tree
I heard a crunch and a munch! Who could it be?

Two little apples hanging on a tree,
I ate one; yes, it was me.

One little apple hanging on a tree,
Willy the worm ate it, you see.

No more apples hanging on the tree,
Better give a call to the honeybee!

4. When the children become familiar with the story, let them take turns removing the apples from the board.

5. Have a conversation with the children about the role of the honeybee in the life cycle of the apple tree.

Reviewing What the Children Learned

✖ Do the children count backward successfully once they are familiar with the rhyme?

✖ Ask individual children the following questions:
Why would you need to call the honeybee?
What other plants might bees help?

More to Do

❋ Expand on your conversation above by placing some plastic flowers in a row on a table or tray. Use the honeybee from this activity to show the children how the bee travels from flower to flower looking for pollen to make honey. Explain that as the bee travels, it spreads the pollen from one flower to another, which helps them make seeds so there will be more flowers.

❋ When going outdoors, count backwards as a way to transition the children to the outdoor area. Line the children up near the door and chant:

> Five little children standing by the door,
> One went outside and then there were four.
> Four little children, quiet as can be,
> One went outside and then there were three.
> Three little children, wondering what to do,
> One went outside and then there were two.
> Two little children, wanting to have fun,
> One went outside, and then there was one.
> One little child, he's the little hero,
> He went outside and then there were zero!

Related Books

Apple Picking Time by Michele B. Slawson
Apples of Your Eye by Allan Fowler
Buzzing Bumblebees by Joelle Riley
The Life and Times of the Apple by Charles Micucci
The Seasons of Arnold's Apple Tree by Gail Gibbons

Five Little Snowmen

What the Children Will Learn

✖ To count backwards from five to one
✖ To listen for rhyming words

Materials

laminating machine or clear contact paper

markers

snowman pattern (see page 159)

Storyboard (see page 21) or Storytelling Apron (see page 24)

sun pattern (see page 167)

Velcro™ hook tape

Preparation

✖ Make five copies of the snowman pattern on page 159.
✖ Make one copy of the sun pattern on page 167.
✖ Use the markers to decorate the sun and the snowmen.
  Decorate the snowmen to create five distinctively different
  snowmen.
✖ Laminate the pieces.
✖ Attach a piece of Velcro hook tape on the back of each piece.
  Note: You can also use art foam for the snowmen. It works
  equally well.

What to Do

1. Use a Storyboard or Storytelling Apron to tell the story to the
   children. Place all five snowmen on the board or apron to start,
   and remove them in turn as you tell the story.
2. When the children are familiar with the rhyme, add the
   motions in parentheses and encourage them to participate.

3. Invite the children to chime in on the line, "Standing in a row." This will become easier as the children become more familiar with the story.

Five Little Snowmen

Five little snowmen (hold up five fingers)
Standing in a row.
The wind blew hard and one had to go. (puff up cheeks and
    blow hard)

Four little snowmen (hold up four fingers)
Standing in a row.
The rain came down and one had to go. (hands overhead, with
    straight fingers as you lower your hands)

Three little snowmen (hold up three fingers)
Standing in a row.
Along came a snowplow and one had to go. (fists together in
    front and push forward)

Two little snowmen (hold up two fingers)
Standing in a row.
Waiting for children, but one had to go. (twiddle thumbs)

One little snowman (hold up one finger)
Standing in a row.
The sun came out . . . (arms above head in circle)
No more snowmen standing in a row. (spread empty hands and
    shrug)

4. When you say, "The sun came out," place the sun on the board above the last snowman. Then pause dramatically and say the last line, "No more snowmen standing in a row," as you slowly remove the last snowman from the apron or the Storyboard.

Reviewing What the Children Learned

Ask individual children the following questions:

* *How many snowmen were there at the beginning of the story?*
* *How many snowmen were left at the end of the story?*

More to Do

* Add cotton balls to the Art Center so the children can make their own snowmen by gluing them to paper.
* After saying the rhyme a couple of times, encourage the children to say the rhyming words. Start the rhyme as you normally would, but when you get to the rhyming word in each phrase (*row, go*), pause and wait for the children to volunteer the word.

Related Books

Our Very Special Snowman by Evalona Mortenson
The Snowman by Raymond Briggs
Snowmen at Night by Caralyn Buehner

Caterpillar

What the Children Will Learn

- About the life cycle of a butterfly

Materials

butterfly life cycle patterns (see pages 160–162)
gold glitter glue
laminating machine or clear contact paper
markers
Storyboard (see page 21)
Velcro™ hook tape

Preparation

- Copy the caterpillar life cycle patterns on pages 160–162. Cut them out and color them with the markers. Use the gold glitter glue to add the gold dots to the chrysalis pattern.
- Laminate the pieces for durability.
- Attach a piece of Velcro tape to the back of each piece.

What to Do

1. Tell the children the rhyme as you place the pieces on the Storyboard. The first time you tell it, do not stop to explain each piece. This will interrupt the flow of the rhyme. After you have told the rhyme a couple of times, you can pause between each verse and talk about that particular part of the life cycle of the butterfly.

   Note: This is a great story for a Pizza Story Box (see page 26).

Caterpillar

Caterpillar, caterpillar fat and green,
Crawling on the milkweed, hardly seen.

Spinning a chrysalis to hide away,
Waiting and waiting for a special day.

Dots of gold glimmering in the sun,
Waiting for the changes to be done.

Creeping and crawling are no more.
Open your wings so you can soar.

Spread those wings and fly up high.
Today you are a butterfly!

2. Place the Storyboard and pieces in the Science Center and allow the children to experiment freely by placing the cards in the correct order. Offer guidance as needed. **Note**: If possible, make two sets—one for your file and one for the science center.

Reviewing What the Children Learned

Ask individual children the following questions:

* *What is the name of the plant this caterpillar likes to eat?*
* *What is the name of the home the caterpillar spins to live in while it changes into a butterfly?*
* *What changes take place while the caterpillar is in the chrysalis?*

More to Do

* Add purchased butterfly wings to the Dramatic Play Center. You can also make wings from poster board and attach them to a story band for children to use in the Dramatic Play Center or the Story Corner (see page 27). Invite the children to decorate these wings.

✽ Create butterfly paintings by having the children use dot paints on one-half of a sheet of paper. While the paint is still wet, fold the paper in half and press firmly to transfer the image to the other side. Open the paper and allow the paint to dry. Cut the paper into a butterfly shape.

✽ Make caterpillar puppets by adding googly eyes to green tube socks.

Related Books

Butterfly House by Eve Bunting

Caterpillar and Butterfly by Ambelin Kwaymullina

First the Egg by Laura Vaccaro Seeger

The Very Hungry Caterpillar by Eric Carle

Where Does the Butterfly Go When It Rains? by May Garelick

Fly, Kite, Fly

What the Children Will Learn

✱ About rhyming words
✱ To relate the stories and poems they hear to activities they might do in their real lives

Materials

craft paper (any color)
kite pattern (see page 163)
large piece of poster board
markers and crayons
child-safe scissors
string

Preparation

✱ Create a large kite using poster board and scissors.
✱ Decorate the kite with markers or crayons.
✱ Attach a tail to the kite using the string and pieces cut from the craft paper.
✱ Print the "Fly, Kite, Fly" poem on the large kite.

What to Do

1. During story time, recite the following poem to the children. Use your voice to emphasize the rhyming words. Have fun with the poem and make dramatic motions with the large kite to act it out.

   Fly, Kite, Fly
   I fly my kite up in the sky.
   I fly my kite way up high.

Fly, kite, fly up in the sky.
Fly, kite, fly away up high.
With a long, long string and a twisty tail,
I watch my kite as it sets sail.

Fly, kite, fly up in the sky.
Fly, kite, fly away up high.

Up in the clouds, puffy and white,
My kite can fly out of sight.

Fly, kite, fly up in the sky.
Fly, kite, fly away up high!

2. Give each child a kite, cut from the pattern on page 163.
3. Invite the children to decorate and cut out their kites.
4. Help the children add tails to their kites using string or ribbon and pieces cut from craft paper. Recite the poem again, using all the kites.

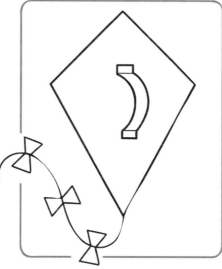

Hint: Attach a handle to the back of each small kite so the children can hold them while reciting the poem, or so they can make their kites fly to some soft, slow music.

5. Post the kites on a bulletin board along with the poem.
6. In the spring, send the kites home with the poem attached.

Reviewing What the Children Learned

Ask individual children the following questions:
* *Where was the kite flying?*
* *What did the kite have hanging down from it?*
* *What else was in the sky with the kite?*

More to Do

✱ Go outside on a blustery day and fly some real kites.

✱ Ask the children to pretend they are kites flying high in the sky on a beautiful day. What can they see from way up there? Record their responses on paper labeled "If I Were a Kite" and post these on the bulletin board with the kites from the activity.

✱ After the children have heard the poem a few times, encourage them to supply the second rhyming word in each phrase. As you say the poem, pause at the end of the second line and ask the children to help you remember the rhyming word. You might say, "I've forgotten what word rhymes with *sky*. Can you help me remember it? What was that word?" The more confused you act, the more the children will be anxious to help you.

Related Books

Angel's Kite/La estrella de Angel by Alberto Blanco
The Kite by Mary Packard
The Legend of the Kite: A Story of China by Chen Jiang Hong

Funny Bunny

Materials

art foam in colors of your choice

fine line permanent marker

patterns of a bunny, squirrel, and duck (see pages 164–166)

pattern of tree (see page 158)

scissors (adult use only)

Storyboard (see page 21)

Velcro™ hook tape

Preparation

✖ Copy the patterns on pages 158 and 164–166, enlarging as needed.

✖ Use the patterns as templates to cut characters out of art foam.

✖ Use the permanent marker to add features to the pieces.

✖ Attach a piece of Velcro tape to the back of each piece.

What to Do

1. Use a Storyboard and the following poem to tell the story of "Funny Bunny" to the children.

   Funny Bunny
   There was a little bunny.
   He lived in the woods.
   He twitched his nose
   Like a good bunny should.

   He hopped by a squirrel.
   He hopped by a tree.
   He hopped by a duck,
   And he hopped by me!

He stared at the squirrel.
He stared at the tree.
He stared at the duck,
But he hopped by me!

That funny little bunny!

2. After telling the story, encourage the children to use Story Bands (see page 25) and the foam characters to retell it to each other.

Reviewing What the Children Learned

✸ Ask individual children to name some of the animals the bunny met.

More to Do

✸ Add bunny ears (either purchased or handmade) to the Dramatic Play Center.
✸ Make small versions of the characters, and glue or tape them to craft sticks so the children can dramatize the rhyme. (Use large characters for the Story Bands and small characters for the craft sticks.)
✸ Duplicate the characters from the activity so the children can use them to create their own scenes and stories.
✸ Encourage the children to add other actions to extend the rhyme. (The bunny might wave, jump, and so on.)

Related Books

Guess How Much I Love You by Sam McBratney
I Am a Bunny by Ole Risom and Richard Scarry
Knuffle Bunny by Mo Willems
Little Bunny Follows His Nose by Katherine Howard
Little Bunny on the Move by Peter McCarty
The Runaway Bunny by Margaret Wise Brown

Weather Watchers

What the Children Will Learn

- About different weather conditions
- The order of the days of the week

Materials

colorful yarn
copies of the weather card patterns (see pages 167–173)
hole punch
laminating machine or clear contact paper
markers
Storyboard (see page 21)
Velcro™ hook tape

Preparation

- Copy the weather cards on pages 167–173. You will want two sets: one on small cards and one on larger cards.
- Use markers to color the weather cards and laminate them for durability.
- Attach a piece of Velcro tape to the back of each small weather card to use the cards with a Story Mitt or Story Band, *or* punch two holes in the top of each weather card and use colorful yarn to create necklaces.

What to Do

1. Before singing this song at story time, pass the weather card necklaces out to seven of the children and have them wear them.

2. Sing the "Weather Watchers" song with the children. Sing to the familiar tune, "Today Is Monday." You can chant it as a rhyme, if you prefer.

3. Perform the motions as you sing. Encourage the children to sing along and perform the motions with you.

4. As the children who are wearing the weather cards hear the name of the day that matches their card, they should move forward to the front of the group as everyone performs the motions.

5. As you lead the song, ask another teacher or an adult helper to put the large weather cards in order on a Storyboard.

6. Repeat the activity as many times as needed to allow every child a turn to wear a weather card.

Weather Watchers
It is Monday.
Monday Sunshine (arms in circle over head)
All you WEATHER WATCHERS (hands over eyes, looking)
It's OK! (thumbs up!)

It is Tuesday.
Tuesday Clouds (float hands above head)
Monday Sunshine
All you WEATHER WATCHERS
It's OK! (thumbs up!)

It is Wednesday.
Wednesday Thunder (clap hands)
Tuesday Clouds
Monday Sunshine
All you WEATHER WATCHERS
It's OK! (thumbs up!)

It is Thursday.

Thursday Lightning (make lightning-
    shaped streaks in the air)

Wednesday Thunder

Tuesday Clouds

Monday Sunshine

All you WEATHER WATCHERS

It's OK! (thumbs up!)

It is Friday.

    Friday Wind (blow between hands)

    Thursday Lightning

    Wednesday Thunder

    Tuesday Clouds

Monday Sunshine

All you WEATHER WATCHERS

It's OK! (thumbs up!)

It is Saturday.

Saturday Rain (wiggle fingers to make rain)

Friday Wind

Thursday Lightning

Wednesday Thunder

Tuesday Clouds

Monday Sunshine

All you WEATHER WATCHERS

It's OK! (thumbs up!)

It is Sunday.

Sunday Rainbows (arch arms to make a rainbow)

Saturday Rain

Friday Wind

Thursday Lightning

Wednesday Thunder

Tuesday Clouds

Monday Sunshine

All you WEATHER WATCHERS

It's OK! (thumbs up!)

Reviewing What the Children Learned

✶ Show individual children the weather cards and ask each child to describe the weather conditions drawn on them.

More to Do

✶ Let the children use any available art materials to create weather pictures in the Art Center.

✶ Keep track of the daily weather using a chart or a calendar. Track the weather for five days, two weeks, or a month.

✶ Place the weather cards and a Storyboard in the Science Center and challenge the children to put the days of the week in the correct order.

✶ Place small cards for this activity in a Pizza Story Box (see page 26). Make two sets of cards—one with just the days of the week and one with just the weather symbols. The children can match the cards.

Related Books

Cloudy with a Chance of Meatballs by Judi Barrett and
    Ron Barrett
Little Cloud and Lady Wind by Toni Morrison and Slade Morrison
Rain by Manya Stojic
Splish, Splash, Spring by Jan Carr
Sunshine Home by Eve Bunting
Thunder Cake by Patricia Polacco

Rooster Waking Up the Farmer

What the Children Will Learn

✖ About the sounds that animals make
✖ To remember a sequence of words and actions

Materials

7 Story Bands (see page 25)
animal patterns (see pages 174–180)
art foam
scissors (adult use only)
straw hat
Velcro™ hook tape

Preparation

✖ Copy the animal patterns on pages 174–180. Use the patterns as templates for creating the characters for this story from art foam.
✖ Attach a piece of Velcro tape to the back of each piece.

What to Do

1. Before beginning this story, use the Storytelling Helper Can (see page 31) to choose seven children to wear the Story Bands. Attach a character to each child's Story Band.
2. Put on the straw hat. You are the farmer in this story.
3. Sing, chant, or tell the following story-poem. Encourage the children to participate by making the animal noises.
4. Ask the children who are wearing the story characters to step forward when they hear the name of their character and lead the group in making the animal sound.

5. As you sing, chant, or tell the last verse, the children who are wearing the Story Bands should move forward and make their animal sounds all together.

Rooster Waking Up the Farmer
by Mary Jo Huff

Hear the rooster waking up the farmer,
Cock-a-doodle, cock-a-doodle, cock-a-doodle-doo,
Cock-a-doodle, cock-a-doodle, cock-a-doodle-doo.

Hear the rooster waking up the animals,
Cock-a-doodle, cock-a-doodle, cock-a-doodle-doo,
Cock-a-doodle, cock-a-doodle, cock-a-doodle-doo.

Hear the cow as the rooster wakes her up,
Cock-a-doodle, cock-a-doodle, cock-a-doodle-doo,
Moo, moo, moo, moo, moo, moo, moo,
Cock-a-doodle, cock-a-doodle, cock-a-doodle-doo.

Hear the donkey as the rooster wakes him up,
Cock-a-doodle, cock-a-doodle, cock-a-doodle-doo,
Hee-haw, hee-haw, hee-haw-hee,
Cock-a-doodle, cock-a-doodle, cock-a-doodle-doo.

Hear the pig as the rooster wakes her up,
Cock-a-doodle, cock-a-doodle, cock-a-doodle-doo.
Oink, oink, oink, oink, oink, oink, oink,
Cock-a-doodle, cock-a-doodle, cock-a-doodle-doo.

Hear the chickens as the rooster wakes them up,
Cock-a-doodle, cock-a-doodle, cock-a-doodle-doo,
Cluck, cluck, cluck, cluck, cluck, cluck, cluck,
Cock-a-doodle, cock-a-doodle, cock-a-doodle-doo.

Hear the horse as the rooster wakes him up,
Cock-a-doodle, cock-a-doodle, cock-a-doodle-doo,
Neigh, neigh, neigh, neigh, neigh, neigh, neigh,
Cock-a-doodle, cock-a-doodle, cock-a-doodle-doo.

Hear the duck as the rooster wakes her up,
Cock-a-doodle, cock-a-doodle, cock-a-doodle-doo,
Quack, quack, quack, quack, quack, quack, quack,
Cock-a-doodle, cock-a-doodle, cock-a-doodle-doo.

Hear all the animals sing their morning song,
Cock-a-doodle, cock-a-doodle, cock-a-doodle-doo,
Moo, moo, moo, moo, moo, moo, moo,
Hee-haw, hee-haw, hee-haw-hee,
Oink, oink, oink, oink, oink, oink, oink,
Cluck, cluck, cluck, cluck, cluck, cluck, cluck,
Neigh, neigh, neigh, neigh, neigh, neigh, neigh,
Quack, quack, quack, quack, quack, quack, quack,
All together the animals can sing.
(Everyone should make a different animal sound and all
sing at once.)

Reviewing What the Children Learned

Ask individual children the following questions:
* *What sound does a (animal name) make?*
* *Which animal did the rooster wake up first / second / third?"*

More to Do

* After you have sung this song a few times, invite each child to
  choose an animal and stand with the child wearing that animal
  character. Repeat the song and have each group make the
  appropriate animal sound. You can then create a graph that
  shows how many children chose each animal.
* Make two copies of each animal pattern, cut them into cards,
  and use them for a memory game.
* Ask the children to name other animals that might live on
  a farm.
* Sing "Old McDonald Had a Farm" together.

Related Books

Barnyard Bath! by Sandra Boynton

Farm Tales: Little Golden Book Collection by Golden Books

Farming by Gail Gibbons

Mrs. Wishy-Washy's Farm by Joy Cowley

Old MacDonald Had a Farm by Carol Jones

Chicken Fun

What the Children Will Learn

✶ To count from 1 to 10
✶ To listen for and recognize rhyming words
✶ To recognize the numerals from 1 to 10

Materials

chicken pattern card (see page 181)
laminating machine or clear contact paper
markers
scissors (adult use only)
Story Bands (see page 25)
Storyboard (see page 21)
Velcro™ hook tape

Preparation

✶ Copy the chicken pattern card on page 181.
✶ Number the chickens from 1 to 10.
✶ Color each chicken so it is different from the other chickens.
✶ Cut out the cards.
✶ Put a piece of Velcro tape on the back of each card

What to Do

1. During story time, use the "Chicken Fun" song to tell a story. Place your thumbs under your arms and extend your elbows to make chicken wings.

2. Sing the song "Chicken Fun" (below).
   Note: This song is on the CD *Chicken Fun* by Mary Jo Huff. If you do not know the tune, chant the song instead of singing it.

3. Have the children repeat each phrase after you. This is indicated by the words "call back" in parentheses. When the children are first learning the song, it is helpful to have another

teacher participate with the children to cue them when it is their turn to sing.

4. Do the motions described in parentheses after each line. Be silly, have fun, and expect lots of giggling. Encourage the children to imitate the motions.

5. Place the chicken cards on a Storyboard as you sing the song. **Note:** Place your thumbs under your arms and flap your chicken wings throughout this song.

Chicken Fun

Chicken one and Chicken two
(Call Back)
Let's all do the chicken chew (extend neck in
    a pecking motion)
(Call Back)

Bawk, ba ba bawk, ba ba bawk, bawk, bawk
(Call Back)

Chicken two and Chicken three
(Call Back)
Let's all climb the chicken tree (hand over hand like climbing)
(Call Back)

Bawk, ba ba bawk, ba ba bawk, bawk, bawk
(Call Back)

Chicken three and Chicken four
(Call Back)
Let's all shut the chicken door (clap hands)
(Call Back)

Bawk, ba ba bawk, ba ba bawk, bawk, bawk
(Call Back)

Chicken four and Chicken five
(Call Back)
Let's all do the chicken jive (extend pointer finger and jive)
(Call Back)

Bawk, ba ba bawk, ba ba bawk, bawk, bawk
(Call Back)

Chicken five and Chicken six
(Call Back)
Let's all do the chicken mix (extend hands and move over
    each other)
(Call Back)

Bawk, ba ba bawk, ba ba bawk, bawk, bawk
(Call Back)

Chicken six and Chicken seven
(Call Back)
Let's all pray to chicken heaven (fold hands)
(Call Back)

Bawk, ba ba bawk, ba ba bawk, bawk, bawk
(Call Back)

Chicken seven and Chicken eight
(Call Back)
Let's all go on a chicken date (pucker up and kiss, kiss, kiss)
(Call Back)

Bawk, ba ba bawk, ba ba bawk, bawk, bawk
(Call Back)

Chicken eight and Chicken nine
(Call Back)
Let's all shake the chicken hind (shake your behind)
(Call Back)

Bawk, ba ba bawk, ba ba bawk, bawk, bawk
(Call Back)

Chicken nine and Chicken ten
(Call Back)
Let's all strut back to our pen (lift legs and strut)
(Call Back)

Bawk, ba ba bawk, ba ba bawk, bawk, bawk
Bawk, ba ba bawk, ba ba bawk, bawk, bawk
Bawk, ba ba bawk, ba ba bawk, bawk, bawk
(Call Back)

Reviewing What the Children Learned

- Ask individual children to count from 1 to 10.
- Ask individual children to supply a rhyming word from the song. For example, ask, "What is a word that rhymes with *ten*?" The answer from the song would be "pen," but any rhyming word the child thinks of is, of course, the right answer. Use the children's rhyming words to change the chant.

More to Do

- When transitioning to the outdoors, lead the children in a Chicken Fun Dance instead of just walking in a line.
- Put the Chicken Fun Cards and a Storyboard in the Science Center and encourage the children to put the cards in numerical order.
- Copy the cards to make a memory game.
- The cards can also be used with a Pizza Story Box (see page 26).

Related Books

Chicken Little by Steven Kellogg
Chicken Man by Michelle Edwards
Chickens to the Rescue by John Himmelman
First the Egg by Laura Vaccaro Seeger
Louise, the Adventures of a Chicken by Kate Dicamillo
One Little Chicken: A Counting Book by David Elliott
Silly Chicken by Rukhsana Khan

Stories by Mary Jo Huff

Playful Frog Tale

What the Children Will Learn

✖ About nature
✖ Sequencing skills

Materials

clear tape
craft sticks
laminating machine or clear contact paper
markers
patterns (see pages 182–186)
scissors (adult use only)
Storyboard (see page 21)
Velcro™ hook tape

Preparation

✖ Copy the patterns on pages 182–186. Color, cut out, and
   laminate the pieces.
✖ Attach Velcro tape to the back of each piece.
✖ Read the story through a few times before presenting it, so you
   can rely more on your memory than on reading the text. Do not

worry about getting each word exactly right, except for the refrain. The children will chime in on this part.

What to Do

1. Before you tell the children the story, teach them the refrain that starts with, "I'm a hungry little frog...," using a singsong voice.
2. Set up the Storyboard and tell the story to the children. Encourage the children to join in on the refrain.

Playful Frog Tale
by Mary Jo Huff

Little frog was sitting quietly on a big, old log. It was lunchtime and he was hungry. He noticed a small lizard sunning himself on the end of the log. He hopped over to the lizard and said:

"I'm a hungry little frog,
And you're bothering my log.
I don't want to fight,
But if you don't watch out
I'll just take a bite."

The hungry frog flicked his quick, sticky tongue and gobbled up the little lizard. He was still hungry. He looked around and saw a fuzzy caterpillar crawling up the side of the log. He hopped over to the caterpillar and said:

"I'm a hungry little frog,
And you're bothering my log.
I don't want to fight,
But if you don't watch out
I'll just take a bite."

With a quick flick of his quick, sticky tongue, the hungry frog gobbled up the fuzzy caterpillar. The frog was still hungry.

He spotted a dragonfly resting on the end of the log. He hopped over to the dragonfly and said:

"I'm a hungry little frog
And you're bothering my log.
I don't want to fight,
But if you don't watch out
I'll just take a bite."

The frog's quick, sticky tongue was quicker than the wings of the dragonfly. The frog gobbled up the dragonfly. The frog was still hungry.

He heard a swarm of mosquitoes hovering close to the top of the log. He quietly hopped near the swarm and said:

"I'm a hungry little frog,
And you're bothering my log.
I don't want to fight,
But if you don't watch out
I'll just take a bite."

Before the swarm could move, the frog swallowed every one of the mosquitoes with quick flicks of his quick, sticky tongue. He was still hungry.

A small fish swam close to the log. The little frog hopped up to the fish and said:

"I'm a hungry little frog,
And you're bothering my log.
I don't want to fight,
But if you don't watch out
I'll just take a bite."

The little fish laughed and dared the frog to take a bite. The frog leaped toward the little fish. That little fish swam away quickly and hid behind some rocks. The little frog swam after the fish but could not find him. As he searched for the little fish, a big fish swam up to the frog and said:

"I'm a BIG OLD FISH,
With a hungry wish.
I don't want to fight,
But if you don't watch out
I'll take a bite."

The frightened little frog swam to the top of the water and leaped up on his log. He was grateful to be a quiet little frog just sitting on his log.

Reviewing What the Children Learned

Ask individual children the following questions:
* *Why did the frog want to eat the animals and insects?*
* *What are some of the animals and insects in the story?*
* *How many things did the frog in the story eat?*
* *Why was the frog frightened by the big fish?*

More to Do

* Put out a tub of plastic figures that represent the characters in the story. Give the children plenty of time to investigate the figures and use them to replay the story.
* Use magazine pictures to create collages of the characters in the story.
* Using plastic figures or the Storyboard characters, have the children count how many things the frog ate during the story.
* Make another set of characters, using the same patterns on pages 182–186. Cut them out, color, and laminate them. Attach each piece to a craft stick to create stick puppets. Put these puppets in the Library Center. The children will be eager to visit

the center and act out the story on their own. Offer help as needed to help the children remember the sequence of the story. If desired, you can use the patterns to create a strip that shows the characters in the correct order and post it on a nearby wall.

Related Books

Foo, the Flying Frog of Washtub Pond by Belle Yang
Frog Goes to Dinner by Mercer Mayer
A Frog in a Bog by Karma Wilson
Frog on His Own by Mercer Mayer
The Icky Sticky Frog by Dawn Bentley
Oscar and the Frog: A Book About Growing by Geoff Waring
Red-Eyed Tree Frog by Joy Cowley

The Stubborn Plant

What the Children Will Learn

✻ That some vegetables are roots
✻ Memory skills
✻ New vocabulary
✻ About cooperation

Materials

copies of the patterns (see pages 187–194)
laminating machine or clear contact paper
scissors (adult use only)
Storyboard (see page 21)
Velcro™ hook tape

Preparation

✻ Copy the patterns on pages 187–194. Cut out, color, and laminate them.
✻ Attach a piece of Velcro tape to the back of each pattern.
✻ Place the ground pattern on the Storyboard.
✻ Decide which vegetable you will use and put it on the Storyboard so the root is hidden behind the ground and only the top of the vegetable shows.

What to Do

1. Use the character pieces to tell the story. As you tell the story, mention occasionally that the vegetable growing in the garden is a root vegetable. Explain that when we eat a root vegetable we eat the part that was under the ground—the root.

2. Encourage the children to chime in on the repeated text.

3. Each time you tell the story, use a different vegetable pattern and review the vegetables that grow under the ground.

The Stubborn Plant

by Mary Jo Huff

On a bright sunny day, a farmer went to the store (*personalize by inserting the name of a store in your community*) and bought vegetable seeds. He plowed, tilled, and planted his garden. He watered it and tended it. Then it was time to harvest his vegetables. He took a bucket to the garden and started to pull the vegetables out of the ground. The farmer grabbed the top of a vegetable and pulled.

He pulled,
and he pulled,
and he pulled,
but that stubborn plant would not come out of the ground.

The farmer called to his wife to come and help. The wife took hold of the farmer and the farmer took hold of the plant.

They pulled,
and they pulled,
and they pulled,
but that stubborn plant would not come out of the ground.

The wife called to their daughter to come and help. The daughter took hold of the wife, the wife took hold of the farmer, and the farmer took hold of the plant.

They pulled,
and they pulled,
and they pulled,
but that stubborn plant would not come out of the ground.

The daughter called to the dog and the dog came to help. The dog took hold of the daughter, the daughter took hold of the wife, the wife took hold of the farmer, and the farmer took hold of the plant.

They pulled,
and they pulled,
and they pulled,
but that stubborn plant would not come out of the ground.

The dog called to the cat to come and help. The cat took hold of the dog, the dog took hold of the daughter, the daughter took hold of the wife, the wife took hold of the farmer, and the farmer took hold of the plant.

They pulled,
and they pulled,
and they pulled,
but that stubborn plant would not come out of the ground.

The cat called to the mouse to come and help. The mouse took hold of the cat, the cat took hold of the dog, the dog took hold of the daughter, the daughter took hold of the wife, the wife took hold of the farmer, and the farmer took hold of the plant.

All together they pulled,
and they pulled,
and they pulled,
and that stubborn (beet, turnip . . . whatever vegetable you are using on the Storyboard) finally came out of the ground!

"Remember," said the little mouse, "you're *never* too little to help!"

Reviewing What the Children Learned

Ask individual children the following questions:

✱ *What is the name of the vegetable in today's story?*

✱ *Who was the first (second, third, and so on) one to come and help the farmer?*

✱ *Who was the last one to help the farmer?*

More to Do

✱ Send a note home with the children asking the families to send in examples of root vegetables. In the note, explain that their children will touch and/or taste each vegetable. (**Note:** Avoid anything that might be a concern for allergic reactions.) Let the children examine the vegetables and compare them to each other. Emphasize that they are root vegetables. The part we eat grows under the ground. Retell the story with the root vegetables that the children bring to class, then prepare the vegetables for snack.

✱ For a rich learning experience, consider preparing vegetable soup with the vegetables the children bring from home.

✱ Start a class garden. Parent volunteers can till the ground and the children can help plant seedlings. (Growing vegetables from seeds can take a long time, so it is best to invest in seedlings.) Some root vegetables, like radishes and beets, grow quickly, so you will be able to harvest them by the early summer.

Note: Raised garden units are available in many sizes, including 4' × 4'. These units can also be enlarged as needed. The raised gardens allow the children to work in the garden soil. They can be made as tall as needed. One garden could be for vegetables and one for flowers to create a comparison and documentation area.

✱ Have the children create vegetable garden collages by gluing cutout magazine pictures of vegetables to brown paper.

✱ Make two copies of the vegetable patterns on pages 192–194 to create a memory game for the children to play.

✱ Enlarge the character patterns. Attach to Story Bands so the children can act out the story.

Related Books

The Enormous Potato by Aubrey Davis

The Enormous Turnip by Alexei Tolstoy and Scott Goto

The Giant Carrot by Jan Peck

Grandma Lena's Big Ol' Turnip by Denia Lewis Hester

Growing Vegetable Soup by Lois Ehlert

Vegetable Garden by Douglas Florian

Vegetables, Vegetables! by Fay Robinson

Farmer's Headache

What the Children Will Learn

* About animal sounds
* A problem-solving attitude
* About sequencing

Materials

laminating machine or clear contact paper

pattern cards (see pages 195–203)

scissors (adult use only)

Storyboard (see page 21)

Velcro™ hook tape

Preparation

* Create story cards by copying the patterns on pages 195–203. Color them, cut them out, and laminate for durability.
* Attach a piece of Velcro tape to the back of each piece.

What to Do

1. As you tell the story, place the story cards on the Storyboard in order.
2. Be dramatic! This keeps the children's attention and gives the story added energy.

Farmer's Headache
Adapted by Mary Jo Huff

Headache, headache! The farmer had a headache because his wife was always clanging pots and pans in the kitchen, and his children were *so* noisy. Grandma was rocking in her rocking chair and the dog was barking every time he came into the house.

"This is too much noise! It gives me a HEADACHE!" said the farmer.

He went to the doctor to get help for his headache. The doctor told the farmer to bring his horse into the house. The farmer trusted the doctor and took his advice. He went out to the barn and brought the horse into the house.

When the farmer came into the house the next day, he heard his wife in the kitchen clanging pots and pans, and his children were making noise. Grandma was rocking in her rocking chair, the dog was barking, and the horse was neighing.

"This is too much noise! It gives me a HEADACHE!" said the farmer.

The farmer returned to the doctor for a new remedy. The doctor told him to bring his cow into the house. The farmer went home and brought a cow into the house. When he came home the next day, he heard his wife in the kitchen banging pots and pans, the children making noise, grandma rocking in her chair, and the dog barking. The horse was neighing and the cow was mooing.

"This is too much noise! It gives me a HEADACHE!" said the farmer.

The farmer returned to the doctor for a new remedy. The doctor told him to bring his cat into the house. The farmer picked up the cat and brought her into the house. He heard his wife in the kitchen banging pots and pans, the children making noise, grandma rocking in her rocking chair, the dog barking, the horse neighing, the cow mooing, and now the cat meowing.

Story Play: Building Language and Literacy One Story at a Time

"This is too much noise! It gives me a HEADACHE!" said the farmer.

The farmer returned to the doctor for a new remedy. The doctor said to get a quiet little mouse and bring it into the house. The farmer brought a tiny little mouse into the house. When the cat saw the mouse, he began to meow and chase the mouse. The dog barked and chased the cat. The cow mooed and chased the dog. The horse neighed and chased the cow.

The farmer yelled, "Stop! This is too much noise, and I have a HEADACHE!" and he opened the door. The mouse ran out, the cat chased the mouse, the dog chased the cat, the cow chased the dog, the horse chased the cow, and the farmer closed the door. BANG!

He could hear his wife clanging pots and pans, the children making noise, and grandma rocking in her rocker.

"AHHH!" said the farmer. This noise was just right. He never had a headache again.

Reviewing What the Children Learned

Ask individual children the following questions:

- *Why did the farmer have a headache?*
- *Which animals do you remember from our story?*
- *What was the first (second, third) animal the farmer took into the house?*

More to Do

✱ Tell the story again. This time, assign roles to small groups of children and give each group a musical instrument to play when their character is mentioned. For example, two or three children could be the cow group and play maracas. They would vigorously shake their maracas whenever the cow is mentioned in the story.

✱ Enlarge the patterns on pages 195–203. Color, cut out, and laminate the pieces. Attach Velcro to the back of each piece, and create Story Bands. Tell the story again, with the children using the Story Bands to act out the part of each character.

Related Books

Dooby, Dooby Moo by Doreen Cronin
Farming by Gail Gibbons
The Farmyard Jamboree by Margaret Read MacDonald
Giggle, Giggle, Quack by Doreen Cronin
It Could Always Be Worse by Margot Zemach
This Is the Farmer by Nancy Tafuri

Story Play: Building Language and Literacy One Story at a Time

Bear Tale

What the Children Will Learn

✳ To stretch their imaginations
✳ New vocabulary
✳ Who, what, when, where, and why story connections

Materials

bear, fox, fish, and hole-in-the-ice patterns (see pages 204–205)
brown yarn or strips of fuzzy brown fabric
brown, red, white, and tan art foam
brown, red, white, and tan craft paper (for "More to Do")
scissors (adult use only)
Storyboard (see page 21) or a Storytelling Apron (see page 24)
Velcro™ hook tape
Velcro™ loop tape

Preparation

✳ Copy the patterns on pages 204–205.
✳ Use the patterns as templates for cutting art foam into the characters for this story.
✳ Attach a piece of Velcro loop tape to the back of the bear character at the point where the tail would join the body.
✳ Cut lengths of fuzzy brown fabric or cut several loops of brown yarn and tie them together at the top to create a bear's tail. Attach a piece of Velcro hook tape at the top of the bear's tail. This will allow you to attach and detach the bear's tail easily.

Velcro Tape

Back of Bear Pattern

"Tail"

✳ Attach Velcro hook tape to the back of each art foam piece.

✳ You can tell this story using either a Storyboard or a Storytelling Apron. Decide which you want to use and get it ready.

What to Do

1. Attach the tail to the bear.

2. As you tell the story, act it out with the characters on the Storyboard or Storytelling Apron.

3. When you reach the point in the story when the bear's tail snaps off, quickly snap the tail off the bear character while you make a loud snapping noise.

4. After telling the story, pass out the character pieces to the children and encourage them to retell the story on their own using the Storyboard.

Bear Tale
Adapted by Mary Jo Huff

Once upon a time, on a brisk spring day, Bear awoke from his long winter's nap and stretched his big furry body. He growled and swished his big furry tail. In those days, Bear had a long furry tail that he curled around himself to keep warm as he slept during the winter.

Bear headed down to the lake to search for some food. It had been a long time since his last meal! On the way, he met a fox who had a string of fish flung over his shoulder. "WOW!" said Bear. "Where did you get those fish? I am so hungry!"

"Would you share your catch with me?" asked Bear. Fox said, "No, you will have to catch your own fish." He told Bear that there were lots of fish in the lake. Bear asked, "How did you catch that big mess of fish?"

Fox said, "Here is my secret. Pick out a spot on the frozen lake and make a hole in the ice. Stick your long furry tail down in the hole and wait for the fish to bite. The longer you sit, the more fish you will catch."

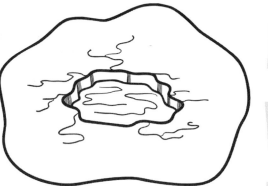

Bear went out on the frozen lake and made a hole in the ice. He stuck his long furry tail down in the hole and waited for the fish to bite. He felt a nip on the end of his tail and then another nip and another nip and another nip.

Bear remembered what Fox said, and decided to sit even longer. He was greedy, and he wanted to catch even more fish than Fox had caught.

Bear sat a long, long time and couldn't feel anything more nipping at his tail. Since he was very hungry, he decided to pull his tail out of the hole and have a fish feast. Bear tried to stand up and pull his tail out, but nothing happened! He pulled harder and harder. He pulled as hard as he could!

SNAP! His tail broke off because it was frozen solid under the ice. And that is why to this day Bear has a stumpy tail. He was just too greedy, and he believed what Fox had told him. Fox was a trickster.

Reviewing What the Children Learned

Ask individual children the following questions:

✖ *What happened to Bear's long tail?*

✖ *Why wouldn't Fox share his fish? Would you share?*

✖ *Do you think this story is real? Did bears really used to have long tails? Could a bear really catch fish with his tail?*

More to Do

✖ Use craft paper and the patterns to create the story characters for the children to take home. Each child should have one hole-in-the-ice, one bear, one fox, and four fish. There is no need for Velcro tape. String the fish together for each child. They can retell the story at home with these props.

- Add bear and fox headbands to the Dramatic Play Center. Cut out rounded bear ears from brown craft paper and attach them to a simple craft paper headband. For the fox, cut out pointed fox ears from red paper and attach to a headband.
- Add photos of real bears and real foxes to the Science Center for categorizing and matching.
- Sing the following song during circle or group time.

Bear Tale Song
(Tune: "Are You Sleeping")

Sleepy Bear, Sleepy Bear,
Time to wake up, time to wake up
Springtime has arrived, springtime has arrived
You can see, you can see

Let's go fishing, let's go fishing
Time to eat, time to eat
Catch a mess of fish, catch a mess of fish
Dinner time, dinner time

Ice on the lake, ice on the lake
Don't be greedy, don't be greedy
Fishing with your tail, fishing with your tail
Fox fooled you, Fox fooled you

- Set up a Storyboard in a quiet area of the room using the characters with Velcro tape. Encourage the children to use the Storyboard and materials to retell the story to each other.

Related Books

Alphabears: An ABC Book by Kathleen Hague
Bear Snores On by Karma Wilson
Bear's New Friend by Karma Wilson
It's the Bear! by Jez Alborough
Sleep, Big Bear, Sleep! by Maureen Wright
Time to Sleep by Denise Fleming

Toby's Big Decision

What the Children Will Learn

* About compass directions
* About the seasons
* To think about decision-making

Materials

laminating machine or clear contact paper
patterns (see pages 206–211)
scissors (adult use only)
Storyboard (see page 21)

Preparation

* Copy the patterns on pages 206–211. Cut them out, color them, and laminate them for durability.
* Set up a Storyboard and tell the story of "Toby's Big Decision" to the children. Place the characters on the Storyboard in the order they appear in the story.

What to Do

1. Use the Storyboard and props to tell the story.
2. After telling the story to the children, ask them if they have ever made a bad decision like the one Toby Goose made.

Toby's Big Decision
by Mary Jo Huff and Jerry Jindrich

Once upon a time, on a cool fall day, a flock of geese splashed down on the pond. It was time for the geese to gather and prepare to fly south for the winter.

"I'm not going south this year," said young Toby Goose as he paddled in the water.

"You have to fly south for the winter, you silly goose!" said his mother, splashing water on him.

Toby had no intention of flying south. He had decided to stay and play with his friends, Bernie Bear, Buzzy Bunny, and Fredonia Frog. He wanted to play all winter.

All the geese had gathered on the grassy bank of the pond, ready to start their journey south. Toby's mom said, "Time to go, Toby. Are you ready?"

"I'm not going," said Toby. "I want to stay here and play with my friends."

"You may not have as much fun as you think you will. All the animals act differently in the winter," said Toby's mom.

"Aw, Mom, we'll have lots of fun!"

Toby's mom looked at him sadly and flew off with the other geese. Toby watched as the geese flapped and honked their way into the sky. They quickly formed a big V and flew out of sight.

He was a little sad, but a familiar voice said, "Hello, Toby. Aren't you flying south for the winter?" It was Bernie Bear.

"I'm not going south this year," said Toby. "I'm going to stay here and play with my friends. We're going to have a good time."

Bernie asked Toby if he wanted to stay with his family during the winter. The cave was a nice, warm place to stay and hibernate for the winter. Bernie asked Toby what he would do while they hibernated.

"While you what?" asked Toby.

"We have to hi-ber-nate," said Bernie Bear. "That means we'll have a nice, long snooze until spring gets here."

"But I'm not sleepy," said Toby. "I want to play all winter, not hi-ber-nate. I'll go see Buzzy Bunny. Have a nice . . . er . . . hi-ber-nation."

Bernie Bear said, "See you in the spring, Toby!"

Toby flew across the pond to find Buzzy Bunny.

Buzzy Bunny popped up out of a hole in the ground and said, "Hi, Toby! I thought all the geese were flying south today."

"Everyone else did," said Toby, "but I decided to stay here so I could play with Bernie Bear and you and Fredonia Frog."

"That's great, but where will you stay, and what will you eat?" Buzzy Bunny said while munching on some clover. "I'll bet my Mom will let you stay with us. Come on in, and we'll ask her."

Buzzy hopped into his hole. Toby forgot for a moment that he was a goose and tried to hop into the rabbit's hole head first behind Buzzy. But geese are bigger than bunnies, so there was Toby, with his head and long neck down in the rabbit's hole, his webbed feet up in the air and his body stuck in the opening.

The bunnies hopped out of a different hole and pulled Toby loose. Toby could see that he wouldn't fit in the Bunny family's house for the winter.

"I guess I'll go over and see if Fredonia Frog is home," said Toby. "I'm sure she doesn't live in a hole. Maybe I can stay with her family for the winter."

"I hope you find a place to stay," said Buzzy. "We could have some fun. My mom lets me play outdoors on sunny days in the winter as long as the fox is not around."

Toby's eyes got big. "What fox?" he asked.

"There's a red fox that lives up in the hills," said Buzzy. "But in the winter he sneaks around here trying to catch birds and bunnies for his supper."

"But I am a bird and you are a bunny," said Toby.

"That's why I can only play outside a short time in the winter," said Buzzy. "And my mom and dad have to watch me while I am playing."

"I don't think winter's going to be so much fun after all," said Toby, and he waddled down to the pond and plopped in for a little swim. He paddled around quietly in a circle for a while, wondering if staying for the winter had been a big mistake.

KERPLUNK! A big splash startled Toby, and a big green face bobbed up out of the water. It was Fredonia Frog.

"Hi, Toby!" croaked Fredonia. "Why aren't you flying south?"

"I wanted to stay here and play with you and Buzzy Bunny and Bernie Bear. But the bear family's going to sleep all winter and the bunnies live in a hole and I can't fit into it. Besides, the fox might eat them if they come out to play," Toby sighed.

"You could stay with me and my family," said Fredonia, "If you don't mind covering up with mud for the winter to keep your skin nice and moist."

"You mean you don't hop and play during the winter?" asked Toby.

"No, the pond freezes," said Fredonia. "It's too cold and I don't like hopping on ice. It makes me shiver! And there aren't many bugs to eat in the winter either. If I could fly like you, I'd be flying way down south where the water's nice and warm in the winter."

Toby was having second thoughts about his plan. He looked up and saw a single, familiar-looking goose flying toward the pond where Toby was swimming.

"MOM!" he cried, "I thought you were gone!"

Mother Goose splashed down beside him and explained that the flock of geese had flown only as far as the next pond.

"I came back to see who you would be staying with for the winter," she said.

"I want to fly south with you, Mom," said Toby. "I don't want to live here during the winter. My friends will be sleeping in a cave or staying in a hole in the ground or covering themselves with mud. Those things aren't much fun for a goose!"

Mother Goose gave Toby a hug and a kiss and they flew off together to the next pond to join the other geese for the big trip south for the winter.

Reviewing What the Children Learned

Ask individual children the following questions:

- *Why didn't Toby Goose want to fly south for the winter?*
- *How do you think Toby felt when he realized that winter at the pond wouldn't be a lot of fun?*
- *Who are Toby's friends? Where do they live?*
- *What does the word* hibernate *mean?*

More to Do

- Make extra copies of the character patterns and give them to the children. They can color them and use them in various ways.
- Add stuffed animals representing the animals in the story to the Reading Center. The children can use them to retell the story to each other.

- Purchase two low-cost blue tablecloths and use them to represent the two ponds in the story. Encourage the children to act out the story together.

Related Books

Blue Goose by Nancy Tafuri
Goose's Story by Cari Best
One Smart Goose by Caroline Jayne Church
Petunia by Roger Duvoisin
The Snow Goose by Paul Gallico

Spider Soup

What the Children Will Learn

* The importance of following directions
* To develop their imaginations
* To follow and remember a sequence of events in a story

Materials

cookbook
large soup pot *or* poster board and marker
magazines (for pictures of vegetables and bugs)
scissors (adult use only)
tape or glue

Preparation

* If you are not using an actual soup pot, draw one on poster board.
* Read the following story several times so you are familiar with it.

What to Do

1. At story time, place the cooking pot (or the drawing, propped up) on a low table in front of you.
2. Tell the story to the children. Pretend to add each ingredient as it is mentioned in the story. Remember to be dramatic and act as if you think the soup is going to be the best you have ever tasted.
3. At the end of the story, have the children shout "Always follow the directions" with you.

Spider Soup

Adapted by Mary Jo Huff

One cool day, Spider decided to fix a pot of soup for dinner. He took a large pot and filled it with water. He put the pot on the stove to cook but he did not know anything about fixing soup. There was a recipe book on the shelf (show the cookbook) and he looked up the word *soup*.

The recipe listed ingredients and how much of each to add to the soup. Spider read the recipe but decided to do it his own way. He did not follow the directions.

First he added a green tomato worm. Then he counted the legs on the centipede and added it to the soup. He added a brown cockroach for texture followed by a small gray rodent, five flies, and a feather. He added a few flower petals to make the broth sweet.

(Pause, and ask the children to name other things to add to the soup.)

The soup had a different smell (sniff, sniff). "Mmmmmmmmmm," he thought, "I'll have Dragonfly join me for lunch."

"Dragonfly, Dragonfly," called Spider.

"What do you want?" Dragonfly asked.

Spider invited Dragonfly to share his soup for lunch. Dragonfly was delighted. Spider asked Dragonfly to taste the soup and check the seasoning. "Does it need anything else?" asked Spider.

"Sl-u-u-ur-rp! GAG! GAG! GAG!" choked Dragonfly. "This tastes disgusting!"

Spider slurped a sip and gagged also. Dragonfly asked Spider what recipe he had tried. Spider admitted that he did not follow directions; he just made up a recipe.

"Nasty, nasty, nasty soup!" exclaimed Dragonfly. Dragonfly told Spider to throw the soup out and start from the beginning. She also told him to follow directions.

Spider followed the recipe for soup. He put in good vegetables.

(Invite the children to tell you what vegetables to put in the soup.)

The soup cooked for a long time and when Spider lifted the lid, he could smell the good soup smell. He took a long sniff. He called to Dragonfly, "Please come and taste my soup; I followed the directions this time."

Dragonfly took a small sl-u-u-u-ur-rp, another sl-u-u-u-ur-rp, and then a big SL-U-U-U-UR-R-RP!

"WOW! This is really good soup!" exclaimed Dragonfly. Spider and Dragonfly sat down and each had a delicious bowl of soup for lunch. Spider never again attempted to cook without following directions. He learned a big lesson: Always follow the directions!

Reviewing What the Children Learned

Ask individual children the following questions:

✖ *What are some of the things Spider put in his soup the first time?*

✖ *What about the second time?*

✖ *What is your favorite kind of soup?*

✖ *Have you ever seen anyone cook by following a recipe?*

More to Do

✱ Make your own soup in the classroom. You can use a slow cooker as long as it is closely supervised and out of reach of the children. Have the children bring in some of the ingredients.

✱ Put a pot in the Dramatic Play Center with a variety of ingredients to make "bad" soup and to make "good" soup. Invite the children to make their own pots of pretend soup.

✱ Cut a big soup pot from a large piece of poster board. Let the children find magazine pictures of vegetables they would add to their soup and glue them to the pot.

✱ Cut another big soup pot from a large piece of poster board. Have the children find pictures of bugs, slugs, and other slimy things and glue them to the pot.

✱ Display both pots on a bulletin board. Label one pot "Nasty Soup" and the other pot "Mmm, Mmm, Good." Post a copy of the story on the bulletin board, too.

Related Books

Duck Soup by Jackie Urbanovic
Mean Soup by Betsy Everitt
Mouse Soup by Arnold Lobel
Stone Soup by Jon J. Muth
Watch Out for the Chicken Feet in Your Soup by Tomie dePaola

Farmer Joe's Garden

What the Children Will Learn

✶ Simple addition
✶ That six equals a half-dozen
✶ To count from one to seven
✶ New vocabulary

Materials

carrot pattern on pages 212–213
large sheet of orange craft paper (11" × 14" or larger)
scissors (adult use only)

Preparation

✶ Fold the orange paper in half and crease it well. Fold it in half again and then again, creasing well each time. Open the folds. You should have eight equal sections.
✶ Refold the paper accordion-style using the folds you just made as a guide.
✶ Cut the top of the paper to resemble a carrot top.
✶ Cut the bottom of the paper to resemble the tapered bottom of a carrot. Do not completely cut the sides of the paper. (See illustration.)
✶ Unfold the paper. You should have eight connected carrots. Cut a carrot off one end so you have a row of seven. (You might want to keep the extra carrot in case you want to add a character to the story.)

4 Folds

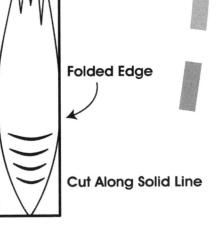

Folded Edge

Cut Along Solid Line

* Color the tops of the carrots green and refold them again, accordion style.
* Read "Farmer Joe's Garden" so you are familiar with the story before sharing it with the children. Be sure to pay attention to the instructions in parentheses. Practice the story, including folding and unfolding the carrots, until you are comfortable with it.

What to Do

1. At story time, tell the story to the children and encourage them to chime in on the parts that feature repeated text such as when Farmer Joe says, "Rabbit, you are such a nuisance!"

Farmer Joe's Garden
by Mary Jo Huff

Once upon a time, there was a farmer named Joe who planted a large garden. He put a fence around the garden to keep the rabbits and deer from eating his vegetables.
Each day Farmer Joe would start work in his garden early in the morning, and at noon his wife would call him for lunch. He always returned to work in the garden until late afternoon.

One day a little rabbit, who had been watching the garden, was hunched behind a large tree stump when he heard Farmer Joe's wife call, "Joe, (stretch out the name Jo-o-oe) lunch is ready!" The little rabbit watched as Farmer Joe opened the gate and headed toward his house. The little rabbit hopped inside the garden and was so happy.

He found the cabbage, lettuce, tomatoes, green beans, and peas. He smelled the onions and then he found the carrot patch. He wanted a carrot for his lunch, but he heard the gate open. Farmer Joe had returned to the garden and he saw the little rabbit. "Rabbit, rabbit, you are a NUISANCE! Get out of my garden!" said Farmer Joe.

The little rabbit was frightened and shaking as he hopped toward the gate. Farmer Joe was standing by the gate holding a hoe in his hand. The little rabbit looked up at Farmer Joe and said, "Tsch, tsch, tsch, (wiggle your nose) Farmer Joe, Farmer Joe, could I have a carrot to take home with me, please, please, please Farmer Joe? (stretch out the name: Jo-o-oe) I love carrots!"

Farmer Joe looked at the little rabbit and said, "Rabbit you are such a NUISANCE, but get yourself a carrot." The little rabbit hopped to the carrot patch and pulled up a carrot. (*show one carrot*)

He hopped back to the gate and looked up at Farmer Joe and wiggled his nose, saying, "Tsch, tsch, tsch, Farmer Joe, Farmer Joe, could I have a carrot for my brother, please, please, please Farmer Joe? He loves carrots!"

Farmer Joe looked at the little rabbit and said, "Rabbit, you are such a NUISANCE, but get another carrot." The little rabbit hopped to the carrot patch and pulled up a carrot. Now the rabbit had two carrots. (*show two carrots*)

He hopped back to the gate and looked up at Farmer Joe and said, "Tsch, tsch, tsch, Farmer Joe, Farmer Joe, could I have a carrot for my sister, please, please, please Farmer Joe? I have a carrot and my brother has a carrot and my sister loves carrots."

Farmer Joe looked at the little rabbit and said, "Rabbit, you are such a NUISANCE, but get another carrot." The little rabbit hopped to the carrot patch and pulled up a carrot. Now he had three carrots. (*show three carrots*)

He hopped back to the gate and looked up at Farmer Joe and said, "Tsch, tsch, tsch, Farmer Joe, Farmer Joe, could I have a carrot for my mama, please, please, please Farmer Joe? I have a carrot and my brother has a carrot, my sister has a carrot, and my mama loves carrots."

Farmer Joe looked at the little rabbit and said, "Rabbit, you are such a NUISANCE, but get another carrot." The little rabbit hopped to the carrot patch and pulled up a carrot. Now he had four carrots. (*show four carrots*)

He hopped back to the gate and looked up at Farmer Joe and said, "Tsch, tsch, tsch, Farmer Joe, Farmer Joe, could I have a carrot for my daddy, please, please, please Farmer Joe? I have a carrot, my brother has a carrot, my sister has a carrot, my mama has a carrot, and my daddy loves carrots. Farmer Joe, my daddy is a big rabbit, a really big rabbit, so could I please have two carrots for my daddy?"

Farmer Joe looked at the little rabbit and said, "Rabbit, you are such a NUISANCE, but get two more carrots." The little rabbit hopped to the carrot patch and pulled up two carrots. Now he had six carrots. (*show six carrots*)

He hopped back to the gate and looked up at Farmer Joe and said, "Tsch, tsch, tsch, Farmer Joe, Farmer Joe, could I have a carrot for a very nice, kind friend, someone who is really, really nice, please, please, please Farmer Joe? I have a carrot, my brother has a carrot, my sister has a carrot, my mama has a carrot and my daddy, he is a big rabbit, he has two carrots, and my friend loves carrots."

Farmer Joe looked at the little rabbit and said, "Rabbit, you are such a NUISANCE, but get another carrot." The little rabbit hopped to the carrot patch and pulled up another carrot. Now he had seven carrots. (*show seven carrots*)

The little rabbit hopped to the gate and Farmer Joe opened the gate. The little rabbit hopped out the gate holding his bunch of carrots. He stopped and looked up at Farmer Joe and said, "Farmer Joe, Farmer Joe, you are the nicest, kindest, most generous friend in the whole wide world. This carrot is for you!" (*fold the carrots to show one carrot*) and he gave Farmer Joe a carrot.

Farmer Joe smiled, and the little rabbit hopped home with his half-dozen carrots.

Reviewing What the Children Learned

Ask individual children the following questions:

* *What did the rabbit want from the garden?*
* *Why did the rabbit want the carrots?*
* *What does the word* nuisance *mean?*

More to Do

* Add orange and green paper, background paper, and glue to the Art Center and let the children create their own carrots or carrot pictures.
* Add a straw hat, farmer overalls, farmer boots, bunny ear headbands, and some play carrots to the Dramatic Play Center and encourage the children to act out the story as they recall it.
* Have a tasting party! Have the children bring in some of the vegetables that grow in Farmer Joe's garden. They should be raw, not cooked or canned. Place the vegetables in small bowls on a table and allow the children to taste the ones they think they might like. Remember to wash everyone's hands and keep the surface of the table clean.
* First Farmer Joe let the rabbit take one carrot and then he let him take another one. Help the children figure out how many carrots the rabbit has at each point in the story. If necessary, use plastic carrots to help the children work out this problem. Once they can answer the one-plus-one question, challenge them to answer another by saying, *"Then the rabbit had two carrots and he got one more. How many did that make altogether?"*
* Divide the children into two groups; one group represents Farmer Joe, the other represents the rabbit. If possible, let one group wear straw hats and the other group wear bunny ears. Tell the story again and ask the groups to chime in on their

characters' parts. A teacher seated with each group will help the children stay focused.

✖ Make carrot salad using the following recipe. Ask a parent volunteer to shred or grate carrots with the children (with close supervision).

Carrot Salad

3 carrots, coarsely grated
¾ cup raisins (for children under age 3, omit the raisins)
½–¾ cup mayonnaise (start with the smaller amount)
juice from ½ lemon
dash of salt and pepper to taste

Combine carrots, raisins, and mayonnaise. Add more mayonnaise if needed. Add lemon juice, salt, and pepper. Mix again. Chill in the refrigerator for an hour.

Related Books

The Carrot Seed by Ruth Krauss
Carrot Soup by John Segal
Number Garden by Sara Pinto
Sensible Hare and the Case of Carrots by Daren King

Shirley and Sam

What the Children Will Learn

✸ About cooperation
✸ About sequencing
✸ About comparative sizes

Materials

large (9" × 12" or larger) piece of orange craft paper
scissors (adult use only)

Preparation

✸ This story is great for the fall season when children are already
  thinking about pumpkins and fall decorations.
✸ Read the story a few times until you are comfortable with it.
  Also, practice cutting out the pumpkins from a single piece of
  craft paper.
✸ Cut out three extra pumpkins of different sizes (small, medium,
  and large) to have in reserve for the very end of the story. Keep
  them near your chair on the floor.

What to Do

1. As you tell the story, when you get to the part of the story
   shown below, fold the orange paper in half and begin to cut
   out a large pumpkin, starting at the bottom, as you say:
   "Sam walked to the orchard, up the hill (begin to cut in
   upward strokes), around the curve (cut the rounded edge of
   the pumpkin), and down to the pumpkin patch (cut down to
   the "V" where the stem would join the pumpkin) and found a
   big round pumpkin."
2. As you say the last line ("found a big round pumpkin"), open
   the folded paper to reveal the pumpkin you have just cut out.

3. Continue to tell the story. When you get to the part where Sam is dragging the pumpkin, move the pumpkin cutout as you speak. Encourage the children to chant the repeated text along with you.

4. When you get to the part in the story where Sam is calling for Shirley to come and help him, use a long, drawn-out plaintive tone as you call for Shirley. Encourage the children to call along with you. You might say, "I'm not sure Shirley can hear Sam. Will you help him call for her? Let's all call for Shirley together." (The children will yell, which is okay.)

5. Continue to tell the story. Each time you reach the part where Sam is going out to the orchard to get a pumpkin, follow step 1 to cut out a smaller pumpkin. Each time you do this you will refold the previous pumpkin cutout in half and cut the new one from the old one. Let the scraps fall on the floor.

6. Continue to tell the story, following the pattern of steps 1 through 5, until you cut out the smallest pumpkin and the story ends. Always encourage the children to chant along and actively participate in the storytelling experience.

7. After the children become familiar with the story, try something different by assigning the roles of Shirley and Sam to two of the children. Tell the story, prompting these two children to say the lines of their characters.

8. Pick up the three extra pumpkins from the floor when the other animals come along at the end.

Shirley and Sam

by Mary Jo Huff

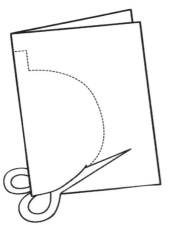

Once upon a time, two little gray squirrels named Shirley and Sam lived in a big oak tree. It was the tallest tree in the forest. One autumn, the leaves were falling from the trees and Shirley wanted to decorate their little nest. Shirley asked Sam to get a pumpkin at the pumpkin patch so they could begin to decorate.

Sam walked to the orchard, up the hill, around the curve, and down to the pumpkin patch and found a

Story Play: Building Language and Literacy One Story at a Time

big round pumpkin. (*Cut the pumpkin as Sam travels.*) Sam took hold of the pumpkin and *dragged* it, and *dragged* it, and *dragged* it back to the big oak tree. He had to call Shirley for help.

"Sh-i-i-i-i-r-r-r-l-e-e-e-y, Sh-i-i-i-i-r-r-r-l-e-e-e-y, Sh-i-i-i-i-r-r-r-l-e-e-e-y!" (*Signal the children to call Shirley.*)

Shirley scampered out on a limb and said, "Sam, that pumpkin is too big to get up to our nest. You will have to go and get a smaller one."

Sam walked back to the orchard, up the hill, around the curve, and down to the pumpkin patch and found a nice round pumpkin. (*Cut the pumpkin as Sam travels.*) Sam took hold of the pumpkin and *dragged* it, and *dragged* it, and *dragged* it back to the big oak tree. (*Signal the children to say "dragged" in a deep voice.*)

He had to call Shirley for help. "Sh-i-i-i-i-r-r-r-l-e-e-e-y, Sh-i-i-i-i-r-r-r-l-e-e-e-y, Sh-i-i-i-i-r-r-r-l-e-e-e-y!" (*Signal the children to call Shirley.*)

Shirley scampered out on a limb and said, "Sam, that pumpkin is also too big to get up to our nest. You will have to go and get a smaller one."

Sam walked back to the orchard, up the hill, around the curve, and down to the pumpkin patch and found a nice round pumpkin. (*Cut the pumpkin as Sam travels.*) Sam took hold of the pumpkin and *dragged* it, and *dragged* it, and *dragged* it back to the big oak tree. (*Signal the children to say "dragged" in a deep voice.*)

He had to call Shirley for help. "Sh-i-i-i-i-r-r-r-l-e-e-e-y, Sh-i-i-i-i-r-r-r-l-e-e-e-y, Sh-i-i-i-i-r-r-r-l-e-e-e-y!" (*Signal the children to call Shirley.*)

Shirley scampered out on a limb and said, "Sam that pumpkin is still too big to get up to our nest. You will have to go and get a really little pumpkin."

So Sam walked back to the orchard, up the hill, around the curve, and down to the pumpkin patch and found a nice little pumpkin. (*Cut the pumpkin as Sam travels.*) Sam took hold of the pumpkin and *dragged* it, and *dragged* it, and *dragged* it back to the big oak tree. (*Signal the children to say "dragged" in a deep voice.*)

He had to call Shirley for help. "Sh-i-i-i-i-r-r-r-l-e-e-e-y, Sh-i-i-i-i-r-r-r-l-e-e-e-y, Sh-i-i-i-i-r-r-r-l-e-e-e-y!" (*Signal the children to call Shirley.*)

Shirley scampered out on a limb and said, "Sam, Wow! That pumpkin is just right! I will come down and help you get it up to the top of the tree."

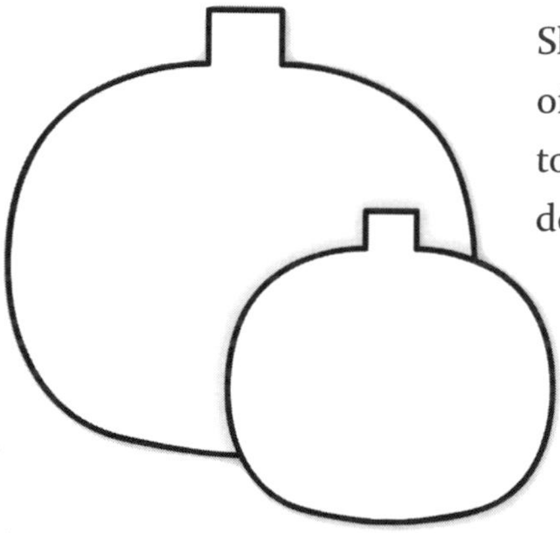

Shirley scampered down the tree. She took hold of one side of the pumpkin and Sam took hold of the other side, and together they took the pumpkin up for a beautiful fall decoration.

Along came Brother Deer. He picked up the biggest pumpkin, Brother Raccoon picked up another pumpkin, and Brother Snake picked up the last pumpkin. Now all the animals had a decoration for fall.

Reviewing What the Children Learned

Ask individual children the following questions:

�֍ *Why did Sam want a pumpkin?*

✖ *Why did Shirley tell Sam he had to go back and get another pumpkin?*

✖ *How many pumpkins did Sam have to drag back to the tree in all?*

✖ *What happened to the pumpkins that were too big for Shirley and Sam's house?*

Story Play: Building Language and Literacy One Story at a Time

More to Do

- ✖ Add three real pumpkins (large, medium, and small) to the Science Center. Provide a measuring tape and scale so the children can experiment with comparing their sizes.
- ✖ Add props to the Dramatic Play Center that will encourage the children to act out the story they have heard. You might add squirrel ears (cut from gray paper and attached to a simple headband also cut from paper) and several small decorative pumpkins.
- ✖ Add orange paper to the Art Center. Encourage the children to cut out their own pumpkins as they chant the lines from the story, "Sam went up the hill (begin to cut in upward strokes), around the curve (cut the rounded edge of the pumpkin), and down to the pumpkin patch (cut the stem end), and found a big round pumpkin." Offer help to any children who seem to be struggling with the task. Children who find it difficult to cut on folded paper can simply cut out a pumpkin shape from an unfolded piece of craft paper.
- ✖ Retell this story in February with red paper for Valentine's Day.

Related Books

The Busy Little Squirrel by Nancy Tafuri
It's Pumpkin Time! by Zoe Hall
Pumpkin Day! by Nancy Elizabeth Wallace
Squirrel's World by Lisa Moser

Appendix

Story Record Form

Name of Story

What the Children Will Learn

Materials

Preparation

What to Do

Reviewing What the Children Learned

More to Do

Related Books

Story Play: Building Language and Literacy One Story at a Time

Seasonal Stories to Read and Tell

Fall

Big Pumpkin by Erica Silverman

The Great Fuzz Frenzy by Janet Stevens

The Little Old Lady Who Was Not Afraid of Anything by Linda Williams

The Little Scarecrow Boy by Margaret Wise Brown

Midnight Farm by Carly Simon

Mouse's First Fall by Lauren Thompson

Pumpkinhead by Eric Kimmel

Someday Is Not a Day of the Week by Denise Brennan-Nelson

Story Time for Little Porcupine by Joseph Slate

Tops & Bottoms by Janet Stevens

Winter

A Big Quiet House by Heather Forest

Cobweb Christmas by Shirley Climo

The Gingerbread Cowboy by Janet Squires

Gingerbread Friends by Jan Brett

The Little Snow Bear by Flavia Weedn

The Mitten Tree by Candace Christiansen

The Snow Bear by Miriam Moss

Snowmen at Night by Caralyn Buehner

Stranger in the Woods by Carl R. Sams and Jean Stoick

Time to Sleep by Denise Fleming

Spring

Chicken Chuck by Bill Martin Jr.

A Freshwater Pond by Adam Hibbert

I Can Be Anything! by Jerry Spinelli

In My Garden by Ward Schumaker

Jubal's Wish by Audrey Wood

Michael Recycle by Ellie Bethel

Mrs. Spitzer's Garden by Edith Pattou

My Garden by Kevin Henkes

Tops & Bottoms by Janet Stevens

A Wagonload of Fish by Judit Z. Bodnar

Summer

Are You a Snail? by Judy Allen

Bad Frogs by Thacher Hurd

Bedtime at the Swamp by Kristyn Crow

Fidgety Fish by Ruth Galloway

The Fisherman and the Turtle by Eric Kimmel

Little Boat by Thomas Docherty

The Rainbow Fish by Marcus Pfister

Rita and Whatsit at the Beach by Jean-Philippe Arrou-Vignod

The Squeaky Door by Margaret Read MacDonald

To the Beach by Thomas Docherty

Recommended Websites

The websites below will connect you to the world of storytelling and the power of language and literacy. Each website is active and filled with information for all early childhood professionals, librarians, teachers, professors, students, and family members.

americanfolklore.net—American Folktales

augusthouse.com—August House

creativekeys.net—Chris King's Storytelling Power

fairy-tales.org.uk—Fairy tales and fables

foxtalesint.com—Brian Fox Ellis

meddybemps.com—101 Story Starters

pbskids.org—PBS for Kids

readingrockets.org—Reading Rockets (enter "stories" or "storytelling" in the search box)

storyarts.org—Story Arts with Heather Forest

StoryBug.net—Karen Chance's webliography of storytelling resources

storyconnection.net—Dianne De Las Casas

story-lovers.com—Story Lovers

storynet.org—National Storytelling Network

storytellin.com—Storytellin' Time with Mary Jo Huff

yesalliance.com—Youth, Educators, and Storytellers Alliance

youthstorytelling.com—Youth storytelling with Kevin Cordi

Patterns

Two Little Blackbirds

p. 53

Hickety Pickety

p. 62

Story Play: Building Language and Literacy One Story at a Time

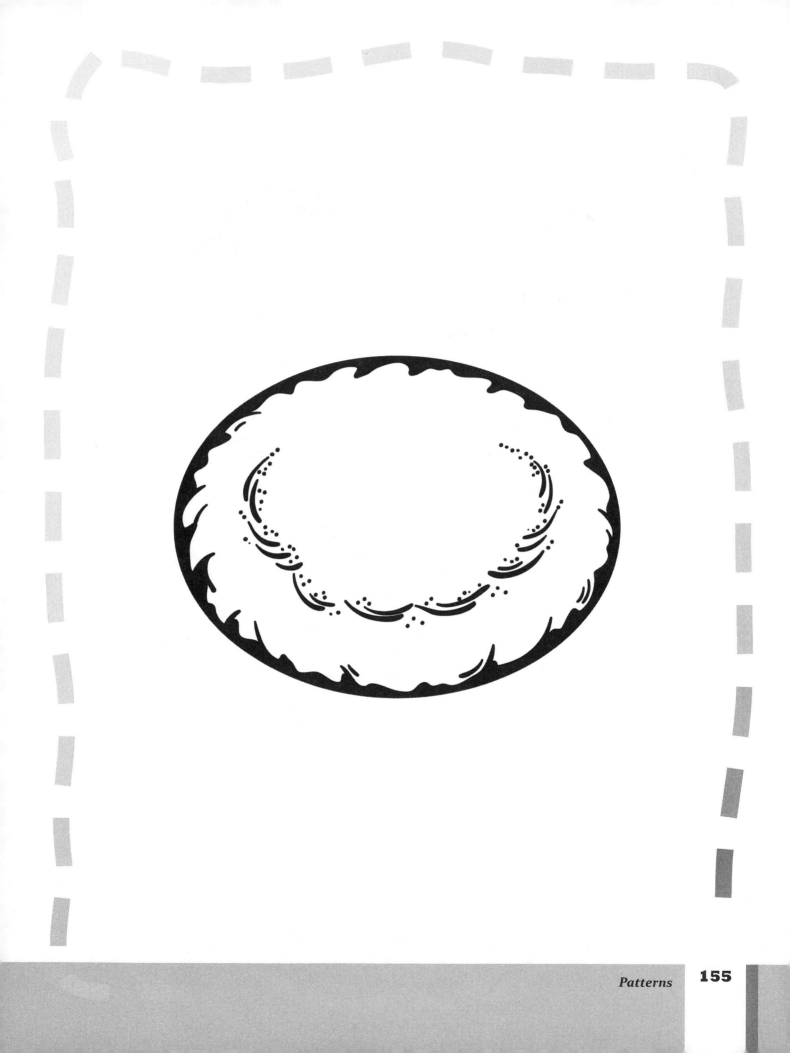

Rooster Call

p. 67

Story Play: Building Language and Literacy One Story at a Time

Gator Hunt

p. 70

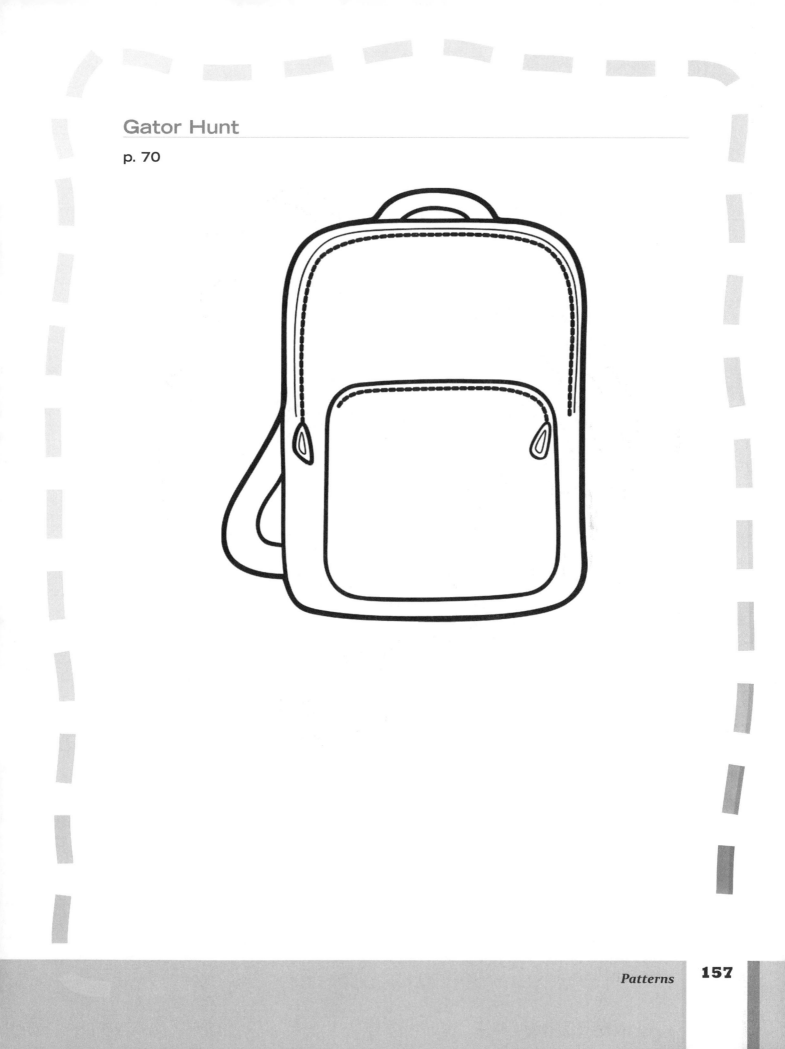

Five Little Apples

p. 80

Story Play: Building Language and Literacy One Story at a Time

Five Little Snowmen

p. 83

Caterpillar

p. 86

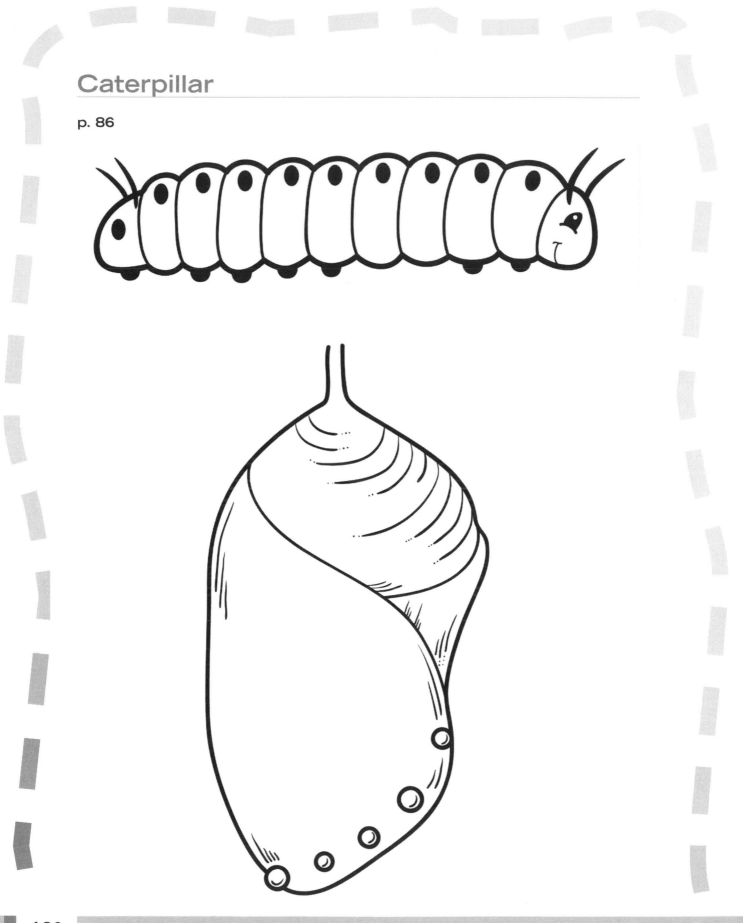

Story Play: Building Language and Literacy One Story at a Time

Story Play: Building Language and Literacy One Story at a Time

Fly, Kite, Fly

p. 89

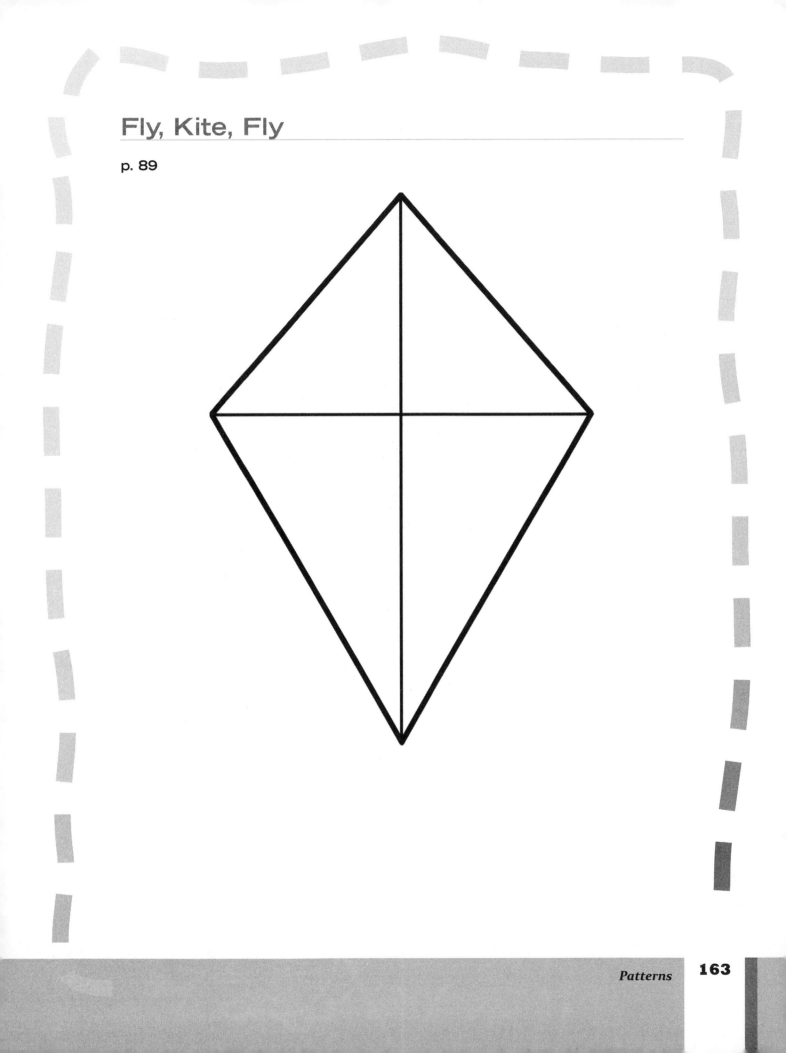

Funny Bunny

p. 92

Story Play: Building Language and Literacy One Story at a Time

Story Play: Building Language and Literacy One Story at a Time

Weather Watchers

p. 94

Story Play: Building Language and Literacy One Story at a Time

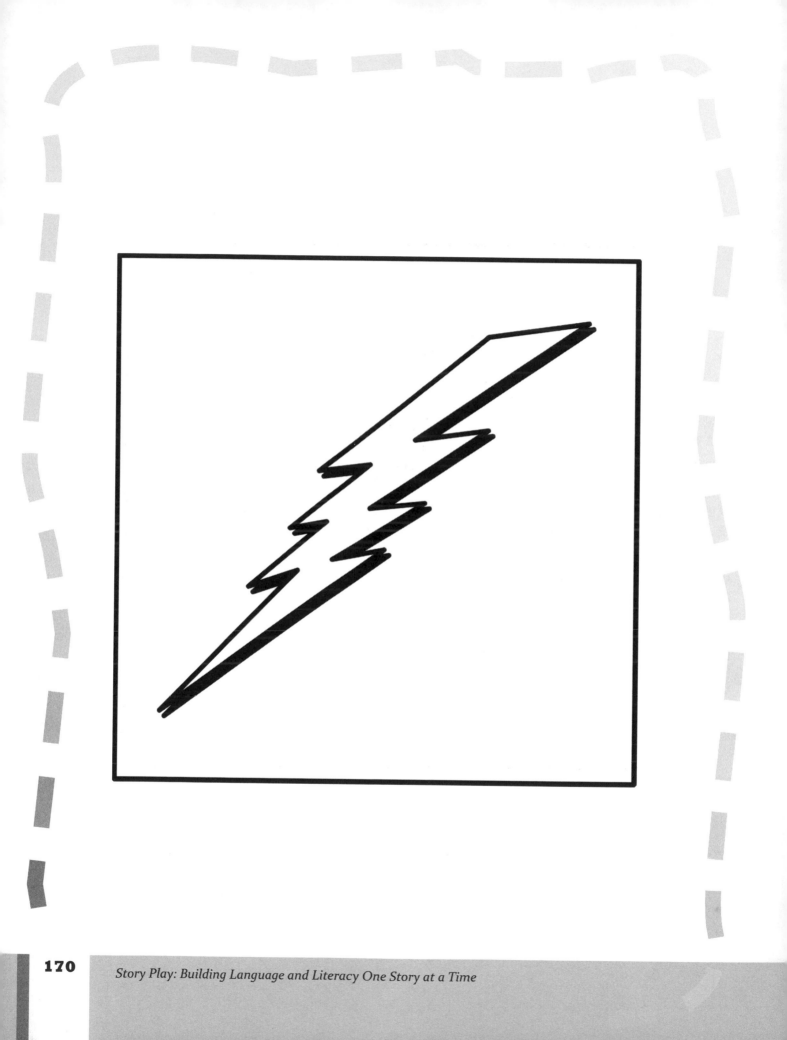

Story Play: Building Language and Literacy One Story at a Time

Rooster Waking Up the Farmer

p. 98

Story Play: Building Language and Literacy One Story at a Time

Story Play: Building Language and Literacy One Story at a Time

Story Play: Building Language and Literacy One Story at a Time

Chicken Fun

p. 102

Playful Frog Tale

p. 107

Story Play: Building Language and Literacy One Story at a Time

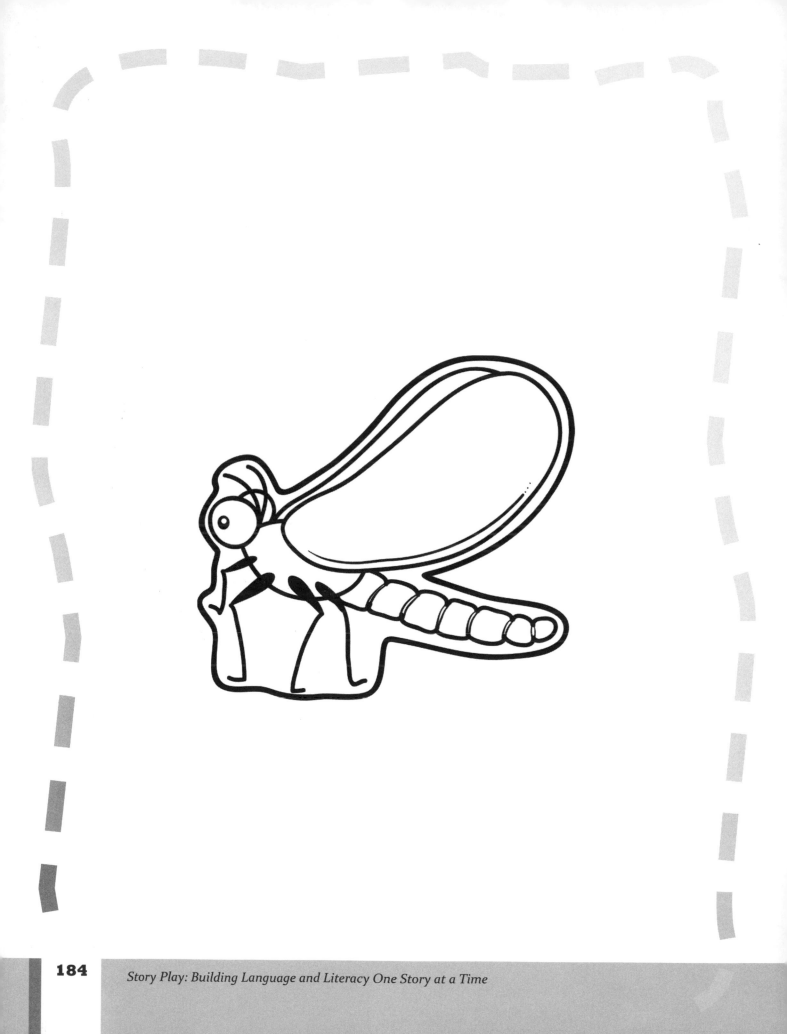

Story Play: Building Language and Literacy One Story at a Time

The Stubborn Plant

p. 112

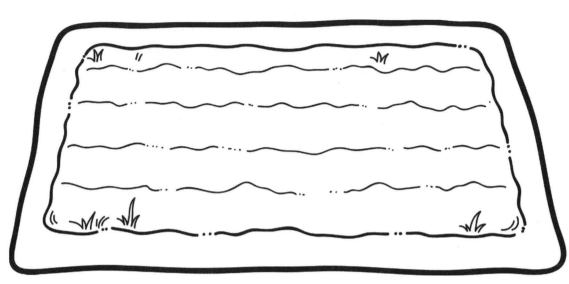

Story Play: Building Language and Literacy One Story at a Time

Story Play: Building Language and Literacy One Story at a Time

Story Play: Building Language and Literacy One Story at a Time

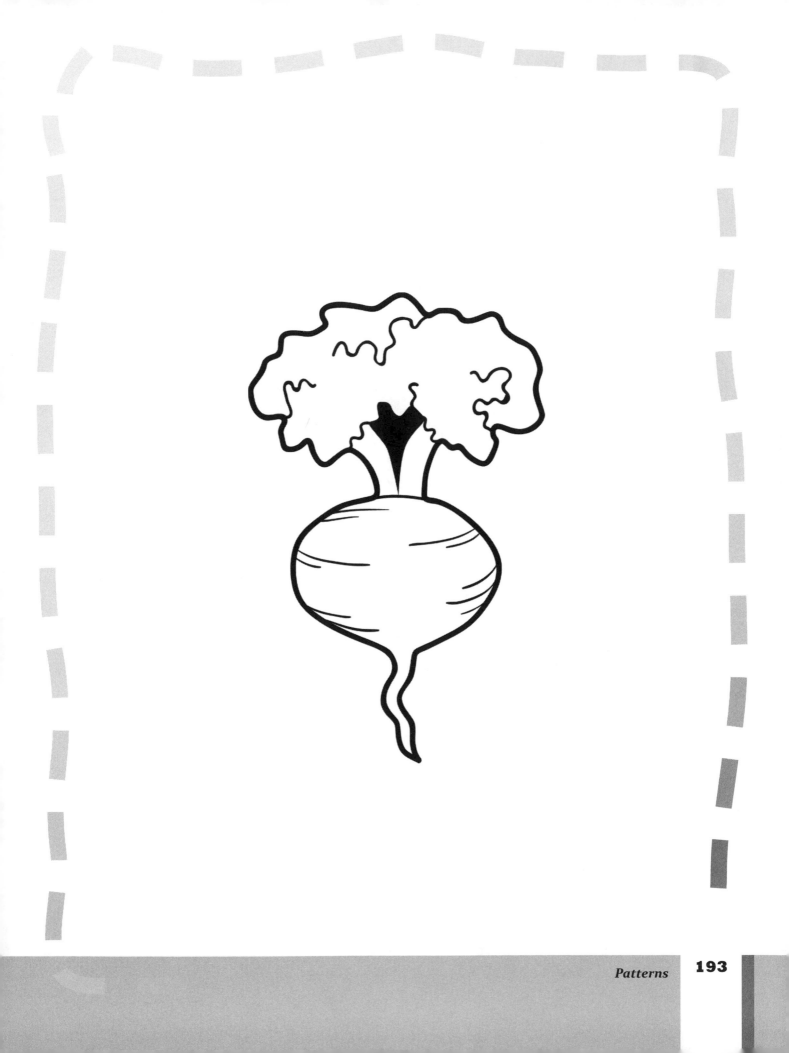

Story Play: Building Language and Literacy One Story at a Time

Farmer's Headache

p. 117

Story Play: Building Language and Literacy One Story at a Time

Story Play: Building Language and Literacy One Story at a Time

Bear Tale

p. 121

Story Play: Building Language and Literacy One Story at a Time

Toby's Big Decision

p. 125

Story Play: Building Language and Literacy One Story at a Time

Story Play: Building Language and Literacy One Story at a Time

Farmer Joe's Garden

p. 135

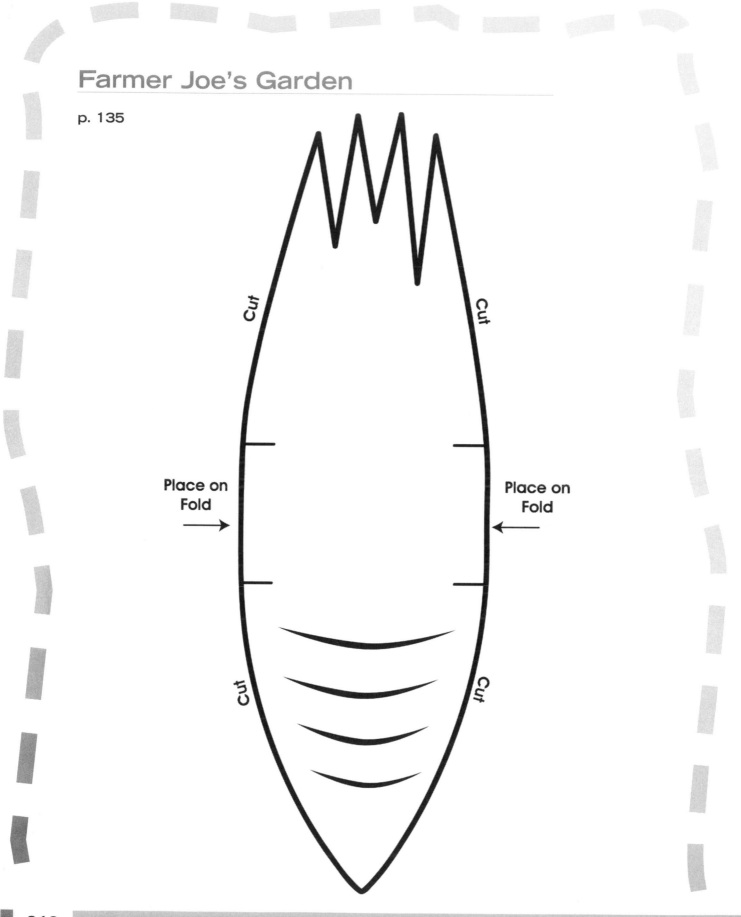

Story Play: Building Language and Literacy One Story at a Time

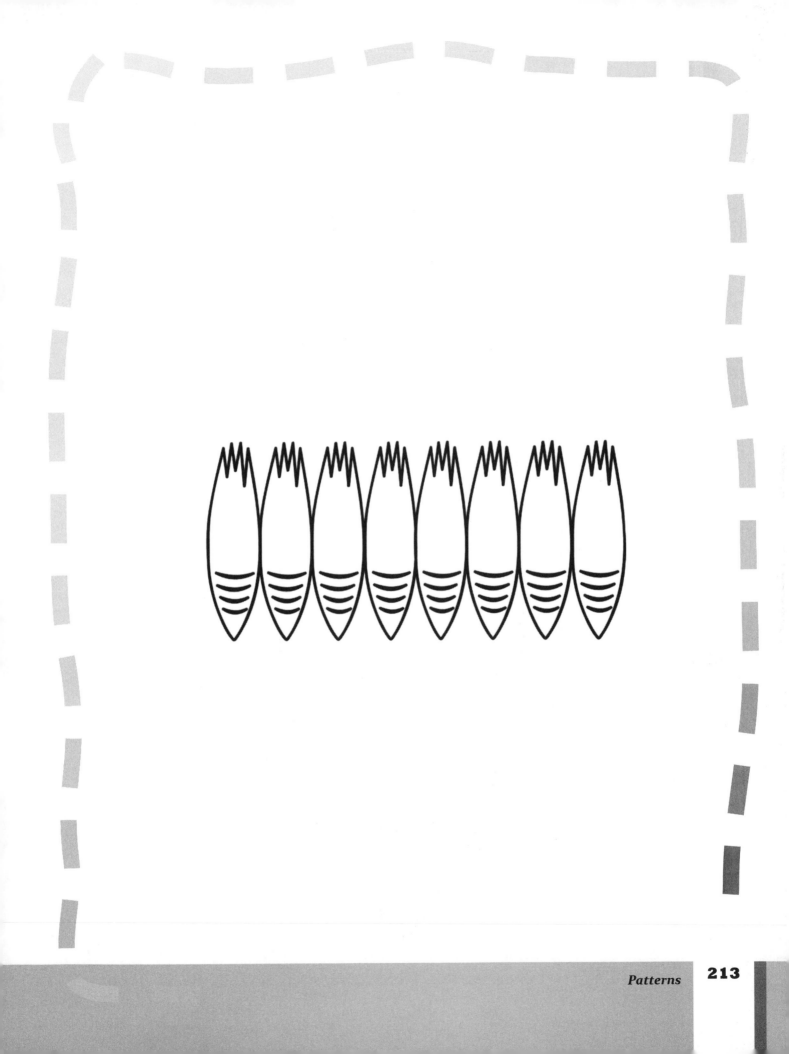

Index of Children's Books

Index